PRAISE FOR *WHEN IS IT RIGHT TO DIE?*

Over the course of several decades, Joni Eareckson Tada has helped us process the hard questions of life. In *When Is It Right to Die?* she does it again—scripturally, carefully, and prayerfully. Thank you, Joni.

Max Lucado, pastor and bestselling author

All across the world, people are swallowing the lie that it's better to be dead than to be disabled or facing serious ongoing health challenges. That's why I'm so glad that Joni Eareckson Tada has written this book. Hearing from someone who has lived with challenges is far more valuable to us than hearing from activists with an agenda.

Jim Daly, president of Focus on the Family

Joni Eareckson Tada has been a champion not only for people with disabilities, but for all people who struggle with pain and disappointment. Always communicating with an assured smile and word of encouragement, Joni has masterfully maneuvered through the difficult subject of dying by shining the light of God's Word filled with peace that overcomes the extremes of life. Your depth of understanding will increase as you exercise your right to choose the joy of eternal life that wins over our few short years on earth. Don't miss reading this one!

Franklin Graham, president and CEO of Billy Graham Evangelistic Association and Sam

Joni Eareckson Tada is not a professional ethicist pondering the theoretical; she is a wise and devoted Jesus follower living out the actual—every day for the past fifty years. *When Is It Right to Die?* offers no easy answers, but it is filled with profound wisdom and eternal perspective and overflows with grace and truth. There's no one I would sooner listen to on this critical question than Joni.

> *Randy Alcorn*, author and founder and director
> of Eternal Perspective Ministries

When we have questions, we want answers—especially when it comes to the tough topics. This means *we all need this book*. It is clear, concise, compelling. What a gift to our world!

> *June Hunt*, founder and Chief Servant
> Officer, Hope for the Heart

Many Christians are committed to upholding the dignity of life at the *beginning* of life, but we face grave choices at the end of life too. We must get this one right—too much hangs in the balance. Thankfully, Joni Eareckson Tada has offered the guidance in *When Is It Right to Die?* Hers is an important and trustworthy voice, and it needs to be heard.

> *John Stonestreet*, president, the Chuck Colson
> Center for Christian Worldview

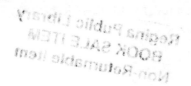

WHEN
IS
IT RIGHT
to DIE?

ALSO BY JONI EARECKSON TADA

Joni: An Unforgettable Story

Diamonds in the Dust

Heaven: Your Real Home

When God Weeps

More Precious Than Silver

Pearls of Great Price

Finding God in Hidden Places

A Place of Healing

Joni & Ken: An Untold Love Story

Beyond Suffering

Beyond Suffering for the Next Generation

Beside Bethesda

A Spectacle of Glory

WHEN

IS

IT RIGHT

to DIE?

A COMFORTING *and* SURPRISING
LOOK *at* DEATH AND DYING

UPDATED EDITION

JONI EARECKSON TADA

ZONDERVAN

When Is It Right to Die?
Copyright © 1992, 2018 by Joni Eareckson Tada

Requests for information should be addressed to:
Zondervan, *3900 Sparks Dr. SE, Grand Rapids, Michigan 49546*

ISBN 978-0-310-34995-2 (ebook)

Library of Congress Cataloging-in-Publication Data

Names: Tada, Joni Eareckson, author.
Title: When is it right to die? : a comforting and surprising look at death and dying / Joni
   Eareckson Tada.
Description: Updated edition. | Grand Rapids, Michigan : Zondervan, [2017] | Originally
   published in 1992 as: When is it right to die?: Suicide, euthanasia, suffering, mercy. |
   Includes bibliographical references.
Identifiers: LCCN 2017032678 | ISBN 9780310349945 (softcover)
Subjects: LCSH: Suicide—Social aspects—United States. | Suicide—Religious aspects—
   Christianity. | Euthanasia—Social aspects—United States. | Euthanasia—Religious
   aspects—Christianity. | Right to die—United States. | People with disabilities—United
   States—Attitudes.
Classification: LCC HV6548.U5 T32 2017 | DDC 362.280973—dc23 LC record available at
   https://lccn.loc.gov/2017032678

Published in association with the literary agency of Wolgemuth & Associates, Inc.

Cover design: Studio Gearbox
Cover photos: © Namning / Shutterstock
Interior design: Kait Lamphere

First printing December 2017 / Printed in the United States of America

To
Jean Swenson
Tawana Grabarz
Debbie Faculjak—
three friends with disabilities
who have helped me find life worth living

CONTENTS

Part Three:
A Time to Die

PREFACE

The last twenty-five years have brought a lot of change. When I first penned the words to *When Is It Right to Die?* much of what I discussed was theoretical. We had begun to see the first signs of the soul-chilling societal acceptance of physician-assisted suicide, but we had to travel abroad to find places where such acceptance of murder had become commonplace. Twenty-five years ago, my hope had been to provide a primer of sorts to readers whose only exposure to euthanasia was the occasional headline.

But in the last twenty-five years, I've ached as I've seen more and more people stand behind the idea that a person has the "right to die." And it gets worse. It is no longer a matter of merely "supporting" a person who has decided that his or her own life is not worth living. No, we are witnesses to more instances where the "right to die" has been given to a person with no say in the matter.

In the fall of 2014, the story broke that a judge in the United Kingdom ruled that, at the request of the mother, food and water should be withdrawn from Nancy Fitzmaurice, a twelve-year-old girl with significant disabilities. This ruling came even *without* a law on the books legalizing euthanasia. It took fourteen days for her to die. Justice Eleanor King at the High Court of Justice read Charlotte Fitzmaurice's plea and instantly declared it was in the mother's and daughter's best interests to withdraw nutrition and fluids that Nancy needed to survive.

This is the slippery slope that advocates and families of people with disabilities have long feared and campaigned against. The mother's request was granted immediately by the UK judge, setting in motion the process of actively euthanizing a person with a significant disability—and the person's only crime was her disabling condition.

Yes, Nancy was suffering; yes, she could not walk, talk, or eat or drink on her own; yes, her disability was severe—but the UK has now set a standard that forcing a person with a disability to die a slow, painful death by starvation is preferable to providing care that would have effectively addressed her pain and discomfort. Surely, the same effort that went into petitioning the courts for permission to remove Nancy's feeding tube could have gone into better pain management therapies, better support, better *life*. Instead, the judge made the determination that Nancy had no quality of life and thus deserved to die.

Perhaps Nancy would still be alive if a peer support community had surrounded her parents. It seems the only people speaking into her life were right-to-die advocates who applauded the judge's decision. To me, this is as great a tragedy as Nancy's death.

And that is why, twenty-five years after I first dived deep into the life and death dilemma, I have returned to this book. As a quadriplegic and as a friend of many special-needs parents, I can testify that their children—many of them with more severe disabling conditions than Nancy—have value. What these families need is not advocacy to legalize something that is not moral. No, families like Nancy's need resources, guidance, and support. They need people to come alongside and affirm that every human being has equal moral value and inherent worth. They need respite and caring communities that provide personal help and a network of compassion. They need to know *true* compassion so they cannot possibly mistake a lethal prescription or a legal death decree as compassion.

And perhaps you do too.

If so, turn the page and let me share with you about life worth living. Let me share with you what death with dignity can *really* mean.

Joni Eareckson Tada
March 2017

SPECIAL THANKS

On this page, I invite you to join me at an awards banquet where you can have a seat at the head table and listen to the accolades. If you're interested, stay and watch the plaques of recognition handed out. The people I'm about to recognize are pretty special.

Francie Lorey, Judy Butler, and Rebecca Olson. These three deserve highest awards. They served as my hands in research and writing. They gave of their time, including Saturdays, to help me complete this book. I'm especially grateful to Rebecca Olson, a writer extraordinaire who serves with us at Joni and Friends. I will always admire the way Rebecca jumped on this project at the last minute, giving it her full-throttle effort.

Dr. John M. Frame. Only after I read his book *Medical Ethics: Principles, Persons, and Problems* was I convinced I could tackle the issue.

Dr. Nigel M. de S. Cameron of Trinity Evangelical Divinity School. His instruction and guidance in ethics guaranteed that this book would reflect sound judgment and solid morals.

David Neff, former editor-in-chief of *Christianity Today*. Whenever I wandered off the beaten path theologically or ethically, David was there to steer me back on course.

Dr. C. Everett Koop, former United States Surgeon General. Although Dr. Koop has long since graduated to heaven, his life and work were my main inspiration. Salt to our culture. Light to our nation. A prophet to the medical society, the legal establishment, the religious community, and to people with disabilities and their families.

Steve Estes and Steve Jensen. Bless you for your help with research and editing. You both know how I feel.

John Sloan, my editor at Zondervan/HarperCollins Christian Publishing. Thank you and the rest of my friends at the publishing house for giving focus, direction, and every resource needed to get the job done. Bless you for believing I had something to say.

Michael and Georgie Lynch, along with the entire Joni and Friends staff. You helped keep things around the office going forward, even when my door was closed and the "Do Not Disturb" sign was out.

The people whose testimonies make up the backbone of this book. My deepest appreciation goes out to you. Your spirit has challenged me to face the moral judgments I must make with courage and conviction.

My husband, Ken. Saving the best for last.

Part One

A TIME
TO LIVE?

LET'S BEGIN HERE

I've never been one for dissertations.

That's just not me. I barely squeezed by in Philosophy 101 at the University of Maryland. Trying to wrap my mind around hard-hitting concepts while my professor read his class notes in standard lecture-hall monotone? Forget it. My mind was already down at the college cafeteria perusing the menu.

Don't give me the War and Peace *version*, I've always thought. *Just answer my questions. Come on, aren't right and wrong as easy to discern as black and white, night and day? Don't confuse me with questions like "Are moralistic codes situational or rigorously rigid?" Just state the plain facts: Is it immoral? Illegal? Unethical? Just tell me.*

Too often I refused to take the time or mental energy to hear and consider, and so I walked away thinking no meaningful answer existed.

Maybe you are like me. It's far too easy to take a casual approach to looking for tough answers to even tougher questions. We go about our days scrolling our Facebook feed, hovering on the edge of heated debates in the employee break room, or strolling down the sidelines of an emotional ethical issue, only catching enough context to form an occasional idea or two. Or perhaps it's not a lazy mental attitude at all. Maybe we're fearful of tough questions . . . or the answers.

What happens, though, when we no longer have the luxury of a casual approach?

A medical report has us up into the wee hours googling to find the medical prognosis for osteogenesis imperfecta. A debilitating accident has us yelling at everyone within earshot, demanding a reason. A teenage daughter downs a bottle of pills, and we stand shocked and defeated, wondering what to do. When tragedy strikes, suddenly the ethical issues pull us in, and we simply cannot be satisfied until we find answers.

That is what happened to me.

A diving accident as a teenager left me totally, permanently paralyzed and in deadly despair . . . a cancerous tumor ate at my five-year-old niece's brain until she withered and wasted away . . . old age and a series of strokes gripped my ninety-year-old father in a web of tubes and machines.

Somewhere between those family tragedies my thinking shifted, and I was forced to face issues I had too long ignored. Ethics was no longer confined to the classroom. Standards of moral judgment now had flesh-and-blood, life and death reality. Why not cut short the suffering, or have someone do it for you if the pain and agony of your disability are too great to bear? Why not leapfrog the dying process and mercifully end the life of a tortured little girl? Why not compassionately pull out the plugs and let an old man die? I had to find answers. That is, if there *were* answers.

I needed answers for more than just my family's living nightmares. My years in a wheelchair introduced me to the world of advocacy and with it to thousands of people with disabilities who were either sinking into or surfacing out of suicidal despair.

Decades of visiting hospitals and rehab centers introduced me to the business executive with ALS (Lou Gehrig's disease) whose body was shrinking and shriveling, the young athlete paralyzed from a spinal cord injury and living in a nursing home, the Vietnam veteran coping with a strange new mental illness, and the teenager with cerebral palsy sitting on the sidelines, feeling as if she were nothing more than an observer of life. Each of these individuals, and thousands more, have been periodically tempted to detour the extreme suffering or mental anguish by escaping into death. And each one asked the same question: *Why not end it all?*

Back when I served on the National Council on the Handicapped under Presidents Ronald Reagan and George H. W. Bush, I quickly saw how politicized these questions were becoming. For those years, I was no stranger to the marbled chambers of government. I listened to the "Why not end it all?" question batted back and forth like a tennis ball between politicians and legislators, doctors and disability associations. Even now, with my position in advocacy less official, I follow court rulings as gavels bang, rendering judgment for what will happen at the bedsides of people who are comatose, severely ill, or disabled. I keep an eye on the headlines every time aid-in-dying initiatives crop up on state ballots.

Behind every news story, every initiative on the ballot, every sign carried by either a right-to-die or right-to-life protester, is a family. A family like mine. A person like me. A person, a family for whom my heart bleeds.

My heart goes out to these people because I have been there. I have lived their story, as a severely depressed disabled person, as a family member, as a friend, as a national advocate, and as a political activist. Their hurts are mine. Their pain I have felt in my own chest. Like them I have searched my own soul, wrestling with the toughest of ethical questions. Questions that do, indeed, have answers.

Although my depression has at times seemed as paralyzing as my spinal cord injury, I have found an answer that makes life worth living. My family also found an answer for my suffering, cancer-ridden niece. And perhaps, most poignantly, we even found an answer for my dying father.

I am convinced that the principles that guided me and my family through the nightmarish maze of depression, suicidal thoughts, suffering, and death can help others. What we learned as a family can benefit other hurting families.

And that's the reason for the book you hold in your hands. Perhaps you are the quadriplegic in a wheelchair or the young mother of a little girl dying of a degenerative nerve disease. You may be sitting at the bedside of an elderly parent who is sinking deeper and deeper into dementia. You may be a friend or family member looking for how to guide a loved one through a dark valley. Or maybe, just maybe, your life does not even touch the world of the terminally ill or dying or disabled. You are just plain tired of living, for whatever painful reason. Your problems have piled on so high that they simply wear you down. Pain has become numbing. Your thinking has become clouded. You are tired, so very tired. Quiet desperation has settled in, and you couldn't care less if there are answers. You only want the hurt to stop.

There is hope. An answer you can live with is within reach. Now, I don't want to come across as one of Job's comforters, dispensing cliché answers that don't fit another person's problems. I wouldn't want to ask you to have the patience of Job to put up with that! And don't worry; what you hold in your hands is not a college treatise.

This book is not about systems of ethics, but about people like you and me and the moral judgments we must make.

Chapter 1

PAINFUL WORDS

*Let those who seek death with dignity beware, lest they
lose life with dignity in the process.*

C. EVERETT KOOP

Fifty years is a long time to be paralyzed. It's not that I'm complaining. I haven't suffered through the usual lung and kidney infections that accompany quadriplegia. With the exception of a few seasons of pressure sores, chronic pain, and even breast cancer, I've enjoyed miraculously good health throughout my decades of paralysis.

But still, after about twenty-five years of living in a wheelchair, I noticed my paralyzed body was beginning to break down. That was a year of blood pressure problems, drastic weight loss, infections, and, worst of all, pressure sores on my sides and back. For three long weeks, two stubborn pressure sores forced me to bed. It wasn't easy lying flat and faceup. And who could guess how long it would take to close those oozing wounds? I'd been in bed with sores before for two months!

In bed, nothing really changed but the days and, occasionally, the sheets. Thankfully I was able to keep my mind active by writing an article or two and a few letters. My husband, Ken, hung a bird feeder outside our bedroom window, thinking the sparrows and occasional nasty blue jays would brighten my spirits. A squirrel he named Mr. McFizz came by daily for the peanuts that Ken tossed under the feeder. The birds and the business of writing articles kept my mind active.

I tried to keep my heart active too. Friends came by. I listened to audiobooks and sermons. I watched a little television. All this kept depression at bay. Well, almost.

Because at times it was oh so hard.

Like the day I began to feel claustrophobic, so hedged in. Being paralyzed, I can't stretch or toss and turn. It's not like I can hop out of bed for a few minutes, visit the fridge, stop by the bathroom to run a brush through my hair, and then climb back under the sheets with a good book. Gravity is my enemy in bed. While there, the only movement I can manage is to turn my head on the pillow. And that summer of pressure sores, after several weeks of lying stiff and still, I felt I couldn't take any more. I had gone through enough.

At that point in my life, I had already survived many years of physical setbacks, and my faith had propelled me long past the bitter denial and bargaining—the stages of depression I experienced when I first broke my neck. But that didn't keep my mind from playing weird games. *I am tired, just plain worn-out from living life with hands that don't work and feet that don't walk. I'm not pitying poor me; I'm just weary and ready to let go.*

I fought back tears and tried to focus on the sparrows fluttering around the feeder. *Maybe they'll cheer me up.* But not so. In fact, for a brief moment, I almost felt envious. *You birds have so much freedom, you can do as you please. No claustrophobic cages. No problems.*

I spent the rest of the afternoon staring at the ceiling, closed off from the chatter of the birds, and listening instead to the drip-drip of the urine that flowed from my catheter tubing into the bedside bucket. My thoughts floated back to the early days of my paralysis in 1967, when I was hospitalized and in bed for not just three weeks but an entire year. My thin, gaunt frame had been covered with pressure sores, and even though I was force-fed, I could not gain weight. That meant even more sores. Thinking back, I was amazed that I had endured an *entire year* of lying flat and faceup.

During that time of hospitalization, my depression wasn't mild or fleeting. I was gripped with the dull, lonely ache of despair. I described my personal holocaust in the book *Joni*:

> Here I was, trapped in this canvas cocoon. I couldn't move anything except my head. Physically, I was little more than a corpse. I had no hope of ever walking again. I could never lead a normal life . . . I had absolutely no idea of how I could find purpose or meaning in just existing day after day—waking, eating, watching TV, sleeping.
>
> Why on earth should a person be forced to live out such a dreary existence? How I prayed for some accident or miracle to kill me. The mental and spiritual anguish was as unbearable as the physical torture.[1]

Decades had passed since I experienced that horrible anguish, and the distance was great between 1967 and that summer of persistent bedsores. But three weeks of lying still, staring at the ceiling and fighting back tears, brought back echoes of that same anguish. Oh, how I longed to be healed of the sores and free from the confines of bed!

The next morning, after Ken left for work, my friend arrived to give me a bath, breakfast, and new dressings on my wounds. Before she went to the kitchen to pour coffee, she flicked on the little TV by my dresser to NBC's *Today Show*. I was relieved when she left the room, which meant I didn't have to interact or force a smile. I was still down—very down.

After the news, the cohost at the time, Bryant Gumbel, introduced the next segment. A shot of Derek Humphry, sitting relaxed and comfortable on the set, flashed on the screen. I recognized him from my years of advocacy work in the disability community. At the time, he was president of the Hemlock Society, a precursor to the Euthanasia Research and Guidance Organization he now heads. Both organizations were formed to promote the idea that terminally ill people should have the legal right to choose the timing of their own death.

Gumbel held up Humphry's book *Final Exit*, the first edition having been published just that year.[2] He tilted it and read the subtitle: *The Practicalities of Self-Deliverance and Assisted Suicide for the Dying*. Even though I had been out of commission and in bed for weeks, I had heard about *Final Exit*. Some called it controversial; others said it never should have been published; and still others insisted bookstores should boycott it. Gumbel put down the book and asked, "No qualms about the possibility that this book could get into the hands of someone who is simply depressed but very curable?"

Humphry argued dispassionately, almost serenely, that he was not promoting suicide, but that dying individuals who wish to achieve a painless death ought to be allowed to plan for it. From his point of view, that meant a person should study suicide options, including different kinds of pills and their dosages, self-starvation, and the implications an act of suicide might have with regard to an insurance policy.

My friend came back into the room and shifted my body closer to the edge of the bed to begin exercising my legs. As she mechanically pushed my paralyzed legs through range-of-motion exercises, I remained riveted to the television.

The interviewer turned from Humphry and introduced Dr. Robert McAfee, a surgeon from the American Medical Association. Gumbel posed a frank and open question, the very one I was thinking: "Do you regret the fact that this book is on sale?"

The doctor shifted in his seat, looking a little uncomfortable. The response he gave touched on the problems every physician faces when their patient is near death. No doctor enjoys seeing someone under their care suffer through pain. And although pain management has advanced considerably, some patients can't face physical discomfort as well as others. It's a tough and perplexing situation for all concerned.

The doctor concluded, "When there's a situation of significant suffering, then appropriate medication to control pain, to hasten the end, may occur."

Gumbel looked perplexed. The doctor's response did not seem at all inconsistent with the premise of Humphry's book on suicide. "So what's the difference?" asked Gumbel.

Dr. McAfee added that a doctor shouldn't do anything illegal. At that point I was as confused as the interviewer. Was "hastening the end" of a terminally ill person's life okay as long as it wasn't illegal? And did making it legal make it right?

After a minute or two, the mini-debate between the author of *Final Exit* and the doctor from the AMA fizzled. Gumbel shrugged his shoulders and said, "Gentlemen, I don't think we have so much disagreement as we do varying viewpoints." The camera flashed to the face of the doctor. He nodded and agreed.[3]

No disagreement? Just varying viewpoints?

Did the three men understand what they had just done? Or said? Or suggested to someone like me? As the morning show moved on to the next segment, I fixed my gaze on my lifeless legs being stretched this way and that. Another hour of a tiresome routine. Each morning the same, day in and day out, year after year. At best, boring. At worst, especially on days like this, depressing.

My mind began to play more games. *Since this television show brought up the subject, wouldn't it be nice to let go, give in? You've earned your Brownie points in that wheelchair, and heaven has got to be better than this. When you're back up in your chair, all it will take will be a quick jerk of the steering mechanism in your accessible van, and you'll be over the side of the freeway. Nobody would even know you committed suicide, and you'll be free of this paralyzed body.*

I shivered and shook the thought out of my head. Yet I couldn't escape the cool, calm rationale of Derek Humphry telling me in his relaxed tone that certain people in certain circumstances should end it all.

After my friend finished giving me a bath and had turned me on my side, I continued the battle with my thoughts. Here I was, a woman of faith, experienced in accepting the challenges of a severe disability, basically very content, joyful, and peaceful when up and about in my wheelchair. Yet here I was, toying with crazy, suicidal thoughts!

And if I could be tempted after listening to Humphry's rationale for the terminally ill, what about the millions of others who watched that interview—who read his book? And not just depressed people with disabilities, but anyone with the Monday morning blues. The three professionals on television may have agreed in a detached way that the disagreement over a person's right to choose their own death was a matter of semantics, but my anguished thoughts said otherwise. I was convinced that mine was not the only struggle.

In fact, not long after that interview on television, I was flipping through *Time* magazine and came to a photo that grabbed my attention—a mother staring vacantly, embracing a framed picture of her son. The article was about a mother's anger over the suicide of her clinically depressed son. He had purchased *Final Exit* and followed to a T the directives in the book. His family's words were chilling: "He became obsessed with the book. It showed him the way."[4]

Obviously a lot of other people, some who were much more depressed than me, watched the same program.

Varying Viewpoints?

A month later, my pressure sores finally closed, and at long last I was able to get out of bed and sit up in my wheelchair. I was hardly the same woman, no longer thinking morbid thoughts. I was amazingly lighthearted and peaceful. How quickly my depression had disappeared!

But I still couldn't get the *Today* segment off my mind. It was that thing about "varying viewpoints." The words the author and the doctor used in the interview kept sticking with me. They didn't talk about someone committing suicide. No, it was a person performing self-deliverance. All these years later, even that term has been pushed aside for others. A physician under a right-to-die law doesn't write out a lethal prescription. No, they administer aid-in-dying. It's not murder; it's physician-assisted death. The phrases themselves seem as cool and detached as Derek Humphry in the interview.

Why the semantic gymnastics? Why the subtle attempt to wrap respectability and sterility around a cold, hard reality? The Death with Dignity National Center, a nonprofit organization dedicated to promoting death-with-dignity laws, makes this argument:

> Physician-assisted suicide, or PAS, is an inaccurate, inappropriate, and biased phrase which opponents often use to scare people about Death with Dignity laws. Because the person is in the process of dying and seeking the option to hasten an already inevitable and imminent death, the request to hasten a death isn't equated with suicide. The patient's primary objective is not to end an otherwise open-ended span of life, but to find dignity in an already impending exit from this world. They're participating in an act to shorten the agony of their final hours, not killing themselves; cancer (or another common underlying condition) is killing them.[5]

Sounds good, doesn't it? Because committing *suicide* and *murder* are still considered socially objectionable. Using these other euphemisms sidesteps the truth and more easily dismantles the long-held ethics that have guided people for centuries.

This is for certain: words have power to persuade. Back in the mid-1980s, one proponent of euthanasia said, "If we try to foist our ideas too strongly and too soon on a society not yet ready to consider them, we will damage our effectiveness. By moving cautiously . . . we gain a larger audience for our views."[6] Now, more than thirty years later, the truth of that statement chills me. The public no longer thinks it's such a terrible idea when a person with a severe disability or terminal illness makes a "perfectly reasonable choice" by deciding to end his or her life. In fact, it is celebrated in movies like *Me Before You*. Here a quadriplegic's choice to end his life instead of accept happiness with the woman who loves him is called courageous and heralded as a "feel-good tearjerker."[7] And worse, the broad acceptance of this idea has resulted in the express legalization of assisted suicide in countries like Belgium, Switzerland, Japan, and Canada, and a growing number of US states.

I couldn't see it then, but back in 1967, when I was one of those severely disabled people confined to a hospital room and surrounded by machines and tubes, my funereal despair was intensified by severe depression. I, or my friends and family, might have been open to listening to aid-in-dying suggestions had we been conditioned by pleasant-sounding persuasion.

"Such a shame, so unfortunate. She'd be better off if she had never made it," one of my distant relatives had sighed. And it almost sounded not half bad. When you can't think beyond four bleak hospital walls, the words of experts and professionals, even distant relatives, can sound plausible.

So I have to wonder what I would have done fifty years ago if I had grown up hearing the theme "better to be dead than disabled" echoing in school hallways, family living rooms, and church foyers. What would I have done if ending my life had been as simple as moving to Vermont or Oregon, or to any of the other states authorizing physician-assisted deaths, and obtaining a lethal prescription?

Two People . . . Two Viewpoints

In the weeks following the interview on NBC's *Today Show*, I dived into the issue of a person's "right to die" with an energy my coworkers thought a bit compulsive. I collected so many magazine articles and newspaper clippings that they were spilling off my desk. But I was curious to see how others were responding to the new book on suicide.

One morning when I arrived at work, I noticed my secretary had placed the latest edition of the newsmagazine *Newsweek* on my desk. I studied the title on the cover: "Choosing Death: A How-To Guide to Suicide Stirs Up a Storm." And another subtitle: "More Doctors Are Helping the Very Sick Die Gently."

Immediately I thought of my friend Bob Ball, a business executive who, until the year before, had served as vice president of a large media corporation. But ALS, Lou Gehrig's disease, changed all that. The last time I saw him, he was sitting in a wheelchair. But soon after, his disease intruded further, and Bob could no longer swallow food. He had a feeding tube put in, and then he was placed on a ventilator. During that time, there were some people who considered Bob's quality of life to be minimal. Yet I knew otherwise.

I knew he was living what was left of his life with courage— desperate for breath, yet uncomplaining; unable to swallow food, but oddly peaceful; only communicating with his eyes and his indomitable smile, yet communicating so much. His friends and family helped him squeeze every ounce of living out of his days. Near the end of his life, they took several hours to load him into an accessible van and take a drive to the beach. On one hand, I knew what he and his family would say about a book on methods of suicide. But on the other hand, I knew Bob would want his death to be gentle, serene, dignified. I mean, who wouldn't want their death to be characterized by dignity?

I flipped open the newsmagazine. The cover title was right. What a storm! The arguments in the articles sounded convincing and compassionate. Helping the very sick die gently sounds worthy. I read the stories of other people whose problems were as insidious as ALS. The story of one woman named Helen touched me deeply. After her husband committed suicide, sixty-two-year-old Helen worked three jobs to support her children and hold on to her home. But a serious heart problem changed everything. Between the many operations, she remained a model patient at the rehab center, cheering on her roommates and chatting with visitors long after she should have been resting.

Even when an operation forced her onto a ventilator, Helen never withdrew from life, delighting in the nurses who fixed her hair and fussed over her makeup. Her spirits remained strong even as her body continued to weaken. Next was the amputation of a leg. Then the other leg. Then Helen changed—it was as though someone robbed her of all her joy. One afternoon she beckoned to a nurse to read her lips and write down a note: "I have decided to end my life as I do not want to live like this. I don't want to make a big deal of this."[8]

The ventilator was removed. It took a little more than a week for her wish to be granted.

Helen's problems were as critical as Bob's, but she held quite a different opinion of her debilitating condition. Helen hated her life. She couldn't have cared less if her request for aid-in- dying was socially objectionable. The hard, cold reality of her impending death was beyond debate. She despised ethical discussion about her situation. "I don't want to live like this" was her matter-of-fact, no-nonsense last will and testament.

As I studied her photo in the magazine, I felt I could read her thoughts. Thoughts that were all too familiar, frightening feelings I had wrestled with just weeks earlier while bedridden with pressure sores. *I am tired, just plain worn-out from living life with hands that don't work and feet that don't walk. I'm not pitying poor me; I'm just weary and ready to let go.*

"Oh God, what have we come to?" I whispered as I pushed aside Helen's picture. "I see Bob's point of view and also . . . Helen's."

Questions for Discussion and Reflection
What Would You Do?

You may not feel prepared for this, but let's jump right into the heat of the battle and wrestle with a hypothetical situation that is actually quite a common experience. So many of the principles you need to make a decision have not yet been covered in the book, but this will help you get a feel for the difficulty that people face. Read the following scenario and decide what you would do in the circumstance described.

A seventy-eight-year-old woman named Charlotte, who is a Christian, has Alzheimer's disease and has been placed by her family in a nursing home. She has severe dementia and does not recognize her friends or family members. Charlotte is becoming increasingly agitated. She is not able to feed herself adequately and doctors have suggested to her family that a feeding tube be inserted to ensure that she receive proper nutrition. The family is divided on this question; Charlotte never made clear her wants and wishes about life supports. Charlotte's daughter wants to say yes to the feeding tube; her son insists no.

Before considering your advice, try to picture what the people in the story might be thinking or feeling. What impact do you think this situation is having on them?

- the daughter
- the son
- the doctor
- the nursing home staff
- Charlotte

If you were the decision maker, what would you do and why?

- side with the son
- side with the daughter

Is there any way to resolve the matter other than by siding with one or the other of Charlotte's children?

Assume that you are close to everyone in the family. Apart from the decision you made and the reasons for it, what would you tell them? Is there anything you would do for the family?

After you complete this book, come back to this section and answer the questions again. Do you notice any difference in your answers? Discuss your decision again and share your differences.

Chapter 2

THE PAIN IS REAL

The point of this life . . . is to become the person God can love perfectly, to satisfy His thirst to love. Being counts more than doing, the singer more than the song. We had better stop looking for escape hatches, for this is our hatchery.[1]

PETER KREEFT

It has been more than ten years since the story captured the headlines, but still in the sphere of disability rights and the right-to-die movement, the name Terri Schiavo carries a world of meaning. Though much has been said about the complicated legal battle over the death of this woman who had severe disabilities, it remains confusing to many.

Terri Schindler Schiavo became disabled after an unexplained collapse and cardiac arrest caused severe brain damage. For most of us who first met Terri Schiavo through television news coverage, all we know of her is her diagnosis—persistent vegetative state (now generally referred to as unresponsive wakefulness syndrome)—and the few images her family circulated of Terri lying in a hospice bed in St. Petersburg, Florida.

And we know of the court cases.

After years of legal skirmishes over her guardianship and care, Terri's husband petitioned the court system to remove Terri's feeding tube, claiming it was what she would have wanted. Terri's parents, Bob and Mary Schindler, fought hard to save Terri's life. During the fourteen years of Terri's disability, emotions ran high as this family's private struggle to save their loved one eventually came under the harsh glare of a worldwide media spotlight. Reporters and cameramen rushed at this weary family as they exited courthouses and Terri's care facility. Advocacy groups from both sides filed court briefs and circulated petitions as Terri's feeding tube was removed and replaced, removed and replaced a second time, and then permanently removed in March 2005. From Florida courts all the way to the federal courts, Congress, and the president, the United States became an audience for the controversy of this family's wrestling with the very real life and death questions of right and wrong in the eyes of God.

The issues were many. Was Terri *really* in a persistent vegetative state? What does such a diagnosis even mean? Could Terri benefit from medical advancements made during the fourteen years of her disability? Did her husband, Michael, accurately represent her wish to never be dependent on life support? In the absence of a written statement of desired care, who can make decisions for an incapacitated patient?

So many confusing pieces—it's little wonder people finally threw up their hands and said, "Oh, let her die." But this case was more than simply "letting" a brain-injured person die. Terri Schiavo was not terminally ill or brain-dead or in a coma; she was disabled. She was capable of interaction with her parents and enjoyed their visits. But she was under her husband's guardianship. He believed further therapies or reevaluations would be futile. Even if authorities doubted the veracity of Terri's state of consciousness and cognizance, reasonable doubt should have been enough to ensure she was kept alive while her case was exhaustively investigated. Even though multiple courts weighed in on her situation, there was never a full rehearing of the facts. Ironically, if Terri had been a criminal, new evidence could have been allowed for review, but that wasn't the case. Instead, with these rulings, a woman with a severe brain injury was denied her rights, and she starved to death.

The Pain Is Widespread

The Schindler/Schiavo family and other families like them captured the spotlight because courts got involved in the decision making. More recent examples of people catching the public eye over life and death decisions include Brittany Maynard, a twenty-nine-year-old who moved to Oregon to die under the Oregon Death with Dignity Act. Both of these stories made headlines largely because of the pull on our heartstrings when we consider a beautiful young woman suffering pain and loss of quality of life.

But these people are the exceptions.

The vast majority of suicides of elderly, terminally ill, or even disabled persons occur quietly within homes and institutions, far from the media, the courts, and the public eye. These are hurting, despondent people who never make the news and only rarely your Facebook feed. These are the ones living a quiet desperation: The woman with cancer, seesawing in and out of remission. The young boy in a semicomatose condition, making eye contact, half smiling, and then drifting away again. The carpenter who broke his neck falling from a second-story window and now, abandoned by his wife, lives in a nursing home.

- Some are terminally ill but not imminently dying.
- Some are elderly and have entered the process of dying.
- Some are in a semicoma.
- Some are suspended in a persistent vegetative state with varying levels of brain function.
- Some are not dying at all. They are just plain depressed because of a mental, emotional, or physical disability.
- And many are the mothers, fathers, sisters, and brothers of these hurting people.

They would squirm in a spotlight. Probably just a few close relatives or neighbors are aware of their desperation. They feel alone and very lonely, afraid to draw too many curious onlookers into their circle of pain. But occasionally they or their families feel compelled to write about their journey of heartache and anguish. And a few of them write to me.

Dear Joni,

My sister Janet, who is twenty-three, was in a serious car accident. She had very critical lung and brain stem damage, and now, four months later, she is still in a coma, mostly unresponsive to life around her. She had a good life with friends, church, a straight-A student, a job as a physical therapist; now it all seems wasted.

If she had lost all her physical capabilities but still retained her mental ability, I could have accepted it so much easier. I'm really struggling with how God could possibly be glorified through this situation. To be honest, it is like

a living death—the grief process doesn't end because Janet
is still "living" . . . I would please appreciate any helpful
information you can send.

Joyce Hutt

I can imagine Joyce keeping vigil by the shadowy bedside of
her sister, wondering, waiting, and hoping. But her letter captures
something far more poignant. She poses an unspoken question:
When, if ever, is life not worth living?

Joyce writes that she is looking to God, struggling with God.
She doesn't want to *play* God by the guardrail of her sister's hospital
bed, arbitrarily ruling that, yes, Janet should die or, no, Janet should
live. Joyce's sister is unable to speak for herself. Who has the right
to say whether or not the life of another is worth living? Perhaps
a few families like the Schindlers/Schiavos or the Maynards can
bring themselves to openly ask the question and then act on the
answer, but thousands like Joyce stand bewildered and confused.

My heart is gripped by her letter. Joyce has poured out personal
and terrifying thoughts to me, a person she hasn't even met. And
tears filled my eyes when I read her last sentence: "I would please
appreciate any helpful information you can send."

It's clear that Joyce and millions like her don't want to make
tragic moral choices.[2] Instead, they want to know what is the right
thing to do. They may not know how to phrase it, but they desire to
understand the difference between prolonging death and sustaining
life. Or for that matter, is there a difference?

How can I best help my family member who is terminally ill?
Or elderly? Or dealing with a debilitating disease? Is it ever ethical
or appropriate to disconnect someone's life-support systems? If
a loved one is dying, can't we just let him or her die? Please tell
me: Is there a difference between withholding medication and

disconnecting feeding tubes or IVs? Show me what to do. Tell me what to say. Give me a tidy list of five easy-to-understand steps. Please, where is a neat conclusion to a painful situation? Yes, please give me helpful information.

What *if* I were to approach Joyce at her sister's bedside and hand her a nicely typed list of dos and don'ts? Would that give her the tools she really needs?

What's more, what if her sister awoke from the coma just long enough to speak her wishes?

She might want to live . . . she might want to die. She might react like the man in the following email:

Dear Joni,

I'm out of hope. [But I am wondering if] you might be able to help my husband, Ron, who was in an accident last year.

My husband is a pastor. The accident left him a quadriplegic. When he came home from the hospital, he continued to pastor from his wheelchair, but then two months later, he was back in the hospital with an infection. And there have been many infections since then and many visits to the hospital. Ron began to become depressed. He has now resigned from his church, and he does not get out of bed.

He doesn't talk. If he answers a question, he only says, "I don't know." He doesn't want to live anymore and doesn't care about our family . . .

Beverly

What can I do? I thought. *How can I reach Ron? Do I send a letter? Books? The name of a local counselor who runs a suicide prevention program? I have to do something. Yet I know it's nearly impossible to sit down with someone like Ron to try to argue with reason and objectivity a case for "life worth living." I've read the professional handbooks of counselors, and they all say the same thing: A person's desire to commit suicide transcends reasoned argument.*

So what good would ten objective arguments against suicide do to sway Ron? I could tell him about my own times of depression, but I'm no longer struggling in severe depression; I see things more clearly now, more objectively. But what does that matter to him? A huge chasm lies between his topsy-turvy emotions and my right-side-up reasoning, his frayed feelings and my coolheaded statements, his insensibilities and my sensibilities.

Still, I had to try. As quickly as I could, I called their home and spoke with Beverly. She tucked the phone under Ron's ear. I could barely hear him breathe, and he was pretty quiet, even though I shared my story, shared some Scriptures, talked about prayer and heaven, and even sang a hymn. This man was a pastor; surely that would break through to him.

Nothing, *nothing* moved this guy lying there in a dark bedroom, shades closed. He only grunted at my encouragements. None of my impassioned reasoning or firsthand experience seemed to stir him.

Suddenly I had an idea. I remembered a scene from a movie. I took a deep breath and said, "Ron, have you seen *The Shawshank Redemption*?" Suddenly, I heard life on the other end of the phone. Maybe the abrupt change got his attention, because he answered! Yes, yes, he had seen that movie. Then I asked him if he remembered a scene at the very end where one character says to another, "Hope is a good thing, maybe the best of things, and no good thing ever dies . . . Get busy living, or get busy dying." I got an answer there too. He remembered that scene. Then I said, "Ron, I want you to join me and ten thousand other quadriplegics this morning who are deciding to get up, get out of bed, and get busy living."

Now, who could have predicted that a scene from an R-rated

movie like *The Shawshank Redemption* would provide the elusive point for two quadriplegics in Christian ministry to connect? But it did, and from that moment, Ron started living again. He went on to become the national prayer coordinator for Marketplace Ministries, and he had a new ministry to hundreds of other hurting people. Ron went on to live another six or so years before complications of his disability took his life. But in those six years, he was able to see his daughter get married and to encourage many, many others.

True, people ready to check out of life, like Ron, can occasionally be talked off the ledge. But many times, rational appeals just don't reach their target.

Helpful Information Isn't Enough

This lesson was driven home through my old friend Ada Walker. Ada was my hospital roommate when I was first injured, and for more than a year, she and I shared a six-bed ward with several other girls. Ada and I were a lot alike. We were young, had been in accidents that left us as quadriplegics, and hated being disabled. We shared our pain, our bitterness, and our horrible fear of what would happen next, who would feed us, how we would be able to bear being dependent on others. Misery loved company back then, and Ada and I would spend long hours commiserating over cold hospital food and dirty sheets.

But that's where the similarities ended. Over the long months of hospitalization, I noticed a change in Ada. Whenever I wheeled past her bed on my way to physical therapy, I observed the difference:

- Ada had given up. I was still fighting.
- Ada had quit. I was steaming mad.

- Ada had glazed eyes. Mine were ablaze with angry fire.
- Ada had stopped going to therapy. I went and worked hard just to prove to those jerky doctors that they didn't know what they were talking about because I *was* going to walk.
- Ada saw no way out. I was ready to bust out the front door of the hospital.
- Ada sullenly shrugged her shoulders at God. I was ready to punch God in the nose.

Her roommates and I were troubled that Ada, during those long reclusive hours, was obviously plotting a deliberate and methodical suicide. Nuts! If I were to end it all, I would have careened off a high curb in a fit of explosive anger.

The numb, lifeless pall hanging over her bed told me she would give anything for pills or a razor. At that point, I was not facing the same suicidal despair. For the moment, anger fueled my energy to face each day, and suicide, as far as I was concerned, would have been a cop-out. Nobody had to convince me of the ethical, right, and appropriate action—it was to break out of that stinking hospital!

By the way, there was one more striking difference between Ada and me. Ada smoked like a chimney. I didn't. I paused by her bed one day. She was puffing on a cigarette that was stuck in a little tray attached to a long tube, the end of which she clenched between her teeth. She inhaled the smoke deeply, as if to split the seams of her lungs. Then exhaling slowly, Ada would wait a few seconds and suck in the smoke again. "You're going to kill yourself with those things," I said, more than a little concerned.

Ada slowly blew out the smoke and watched it rise. "Can't wait," she coolly replied.

"Ada, you can't be serious. Hey, we're not going to let you take the easy way out," I said, half joking as I looked around at our roommates.

Stony silence.

"Look," I said, wheeling closer to her bedside, "your parents would really take it hard."

She turned her head on the pillow and puffed further on her cigarette.

My friend, in spite of my best efforts to dispense helpful information, had made the judgment call. My feeble efforts at being objective fell flat. Life, Ada dispassionately believed, was not worth living. Years later, a lung infection sealed her decision.

Ada's story is bittersweet. Bitter in that she purposefully abused her body in order to engineer an early death. Sweet in that perhaps a year or so before her death, Ada finally crossed that huge chasm between despair and hope and found life worth living. In that final year, she crossed the seemingly unbridgeable gulf from hopelessness to hope. Her topsy-turvy emotions turned right side up.

Whenever I returned to the hospital for a checkup, I always made certain to spend time with Ada. I would sit across from her, amazed. She had become one of the liveliest, most buoyant people I knew, inspiring and encouraging all of her old roommates and everyone else from the janitor to nursing supervisors.

But her spirit could not overrule the damage that had been done to her body. Not even new hope was able to short-circuit the death fuse she had ignited years earlier.

For Ada, even if information *is* what finally helped her over her suicidal despair, it arrived too late.

Questions for Discussion and Reflection
What Is the Right Thing to Do?

1. This chapter poses some agonizing questions for individuals and families facing life and death situations. Can you think of other questions people might face in addition to these?

2. Have you ever had to face the kinds of questions and the kinds of heartache and suffering described in this chapter? If so, share your experiences with others in your group.

3. Talk about practical ways to encourage individuals and families who face these struggles. Are there people in your life who need a word of hope from you today?

Chapter 3

WHY NOT DIE?

Without the incarnation, God is removed from all the pain and all the suffering of the world at its worst . . . [So] we have nothing to say to the person who lies increasingly gaunt, suffering from the encroachment of cancer. We have nothing at all to say if Jesus Christ is not the incarnate God. Because if He is not the incarnate God, what we have in Jesus is simply God's condolences through a representative. Without the incarnation, God does not enter in and share His people's sufferings.

ALISTAIR BEGG

Each year, more than forty-four thousand people die by suicide in the United States. It is estimated that twenty-five times that number *attempt* suicide each year. And the numbers have steadily risen since 2006.[1] Add to that the number of individuals who have chosen physician-assisted suicide—in 2015, 301 people died under Death with Dignity acts in the states of Oregon and Washington alone[2]—and we're facing a *lot* of people who have answered "Why not die?" with an empty silence.

Is that the answer? Is it right to die when a person sees no hope? Is it right to die when the pain becomes excessive, the medical costs prohibitive, the personal dignity shattered? Is it right to die when life becomes too burdensome? Where should the line be drawn? And who has the right to draw it? When is it right to say, "This much I can take, and no more!"

In a way, are we each kind of like the surge protector in my office? It has six electrical outlets. A plug for my computer, and one for the extra monitor my assistant uses when she sits with me. Another for the printer. Another for my desk phone. Another for my desk lamp. And, of course, the plug for the little space heater I keep handy during the winter. This much it takes, and no more. I don't dare plug another surge protector into the first and daisy-chain them so I can charge my headset, mobile phone, and tablet too. The IT staff in my office would have my head. Plus, who knows what electrical nightmares I would cause!

Are people like that? *A terminal illness. Add to it chemotherapy. Then add radiation treatments. Then another surgery. Perhaps another. More treatment. And then something snaps. All their strength drains, and they simply can't take it anymore.*

Is that how it goes? Do we each have the right to choose the timing of our own death depending on our tolerance for pain, expense, and indignity? Of this much I am certain: There is for each of us a time to die, and when that time comes, we should be prepared to go. But the problem remains: Exactly when is it time?

When Is It Right to Die?
"It's None of Your Business."

You want a time? I'll give you a time, I could almost hear Arlene say.
It's when you *decide. Period.*

Arlene Randolph was athletic and full of life, but a fall during
a hiking trip in the coastal mountains of California damaged her
spinal cord. She became severely paralyzed. Doctors kept telling
her that her life would brighten as soon as she learned to sit up . . .
as soon as she got a better wheelchair . . . as soon as she had a
special-order bed brought in . . . as soon as she got to go home. Life
for Arlene didn't happen that neatly or cleanly. As her husband,
Phil, put it, "Everything that could go wrong did go wrong for her."

A self-directed young woman, Arlene knew whose life it was—
her own. It wasn't her husband's, and it wasn't her two children's.
Her life was not owned by the doctors and nurses at the hospital.
She was a firm believer in personal autonomy, and the life and
death choices she contemplated certainly weren't the business of her
rabbi or of the pastor who ran the support group in her community.

Less than a year into her disability, Arlene made a decision.
Unwilling to face a life without hands that worked or feet that
walked, she decided to starve herself to death. Her husband stood
with her and her decision. "She was set in her ways, and that's
the way she's always been. And she was not depressed," her husband said.

I knew Arlene's disability was not a terminal illness and that
she was far from death's door. She was, like me, disabled, and her
decision was a deliberate suicide. Knowing about the physical pain
that accompanies starvation, I sent her a letter.

"Maybe our situations aren't exactly the same," I wrote, "but

I can understand the loneliness, the confusion, the battle with resentment, and the many questions."

As a fellow person with disabilities, I pleaded with her to reconsider. But Arlene died not long after she received my letter.

I talked with Phil on the phone after his wife's death. "Do you wish Arlene would have waited a little longer before she decided to kill herself?" I asked.

There was silence on the other end, and then a tentative "Yes. Yes. I think about it all the time." Then Phil was quick to add, "But it wasn't my choice to stop her. In fact, all of us, the whole family, supported her."

Arlene's death was her own business. That's what she believed anyway. And even though pain management and provisions for independent living are better than ever for people with disabilities, things like customized wheelchairs, special-order beds, attendant care, adapted home environments, and financial aid are, to some people, window dressing. The hard-boiled truth is that they just don't want to live with a severe disabling condition, and they believe the decision to die belongs to them alone.

I can't help but picture Arlene's life before her accident. It's easy to imagine her climbing the cliffs of Big Sur, blazing a trail into the wilderness, or powering ahead on her bicycle, leaving the pack in the dust. And in a way, her choice to die fit her do-it-yourself profile. After all, Arlene was obviously a first-class individual, a born-and-bred American who held on to her individualism tightly as a highly prized value. Her brand of private initiative found its logical and ultimate expression in her decision to die. And in our society, which regards individualism as a valued trait, Arlene's choice seems common, acceptable, and not surprising.

But was Arlene's demise her business and hers alone? To make a decision before life involuntarily leaves us is a decision we do have the power to make. But is it a decision we *should* make? Can it possibly be the best decision for us when it hurts those around us—even if, like Arlene's husband, Phil—they support the decision?

When Is It Right to Die?
"When It's Too Expensive to Live."

"Hey, for a lot of people death is just plain cheaper than life!"

I never would have dreamed that this would be the perspective on the minds of most people at a banquet attended by Christian health care professionals. I was invited to present the main address, and the topic was "Assisted Suicide in the Disability Community." During the Q&A time, the concern turned to rising health care costs. One doctor shook his head and said, "Costs for treatment are soaring beyond what anyone can handle." He tapped his fingers on the table and added, "I think this whole life and death debate is going to be settled by economics."

I shivered. I thought of the subtle pressure that society places on dying, terminally ill, or medically complex people, reminding them that expensive treatment does, after all, have its limits. An example? The Prioritized List of Health Services is used to determine which medical services will be covered by Oregon's state health plan (Medicare/Medicaid). When the program began in the early 1990s, 745 possible categories of treatment were available to enrollees. Ten years ago, the number of covered services had dropped to 503 out of a total of 680 categories of treatment listed. As of January 2017, only 475 of 665 categories are covered.[3]

Are we to the point where health care costs and arguments over insurance coverage have forced us to put a different price tag on each person's life? What about those who are the most economically vulnerable? A decision to forgo treatment and hasten a quick death may be one of a few options for wealthy or well-insured persons, but it could be the *only* option for people who are poor, abandoned, or severely disabled. More than 60 percent of reported deaths under Oregon's Death with Dignity Act in 2015 were individuals on Medicare, Medicaid, or another governmental insurance.[4]

When Is It Right to Die?
"When Death Is Easier Than Facing Life."

There's a time when life is the foe, and death is the friend—that's what Ken Bergstedt came to believe.

A black mustache and beard. A black shirt. Black trousers, shoes, and socks. That was the first thing I noticed about Ken when his father wheeled him into my office. But our conversation was surprisingly lighthearted. While his father sat on the office sofa, Ken and I gabbed about our disabilities, how irked we were with wheelchair manufacturers that kept hiking prices, and how it was a good idea to always double-rinse the sheepskins we slept on. Our one-hour appointment passed quickly. Ken and his dad returned to their RV, and a day later headed back to their home in Las Vegas.

After Ken left, I mused over our similarities and differences. We were old veterans when it came to our disabilities, but we were quite different when it came to our faith. My limitations had forged a stronger faith. His limitations had drained him of any spiritual notions. But I was grateful he kept in touch. I received a letter a couple of months later in which Ken included a few photos of how his dad had modified their RV for his wheelchair.

A year later, I read about Ken in the news. The article was cut-and-dried, explaining that Kenneth Bergstedt, a ventilator-dependent Nevada man, now wished his father to assist him in suicide. Ken's decision was exacerbated by the fear that his dad would soon pass away due to failing health. Both were afraid that Ken would not be adequately cared for once his dad died.

It was virtually impossible to get through to Ken once the news media got involved. Nevertheless, I tried to contact him, writing, "Is it true you said in an article that you have 'no happy or encouraging expectations to look for from life,' and you 'live with constant fears and apprehensions'? Those words are chilling—they remind me of a time when I said the same. But don't have them pull you off the ventilator."

I don't think my letter ever reached him. And from reading further accounts in the news, it was clear why Ken wanted his father to kill him. Life seemed more frightening than death.

Four months later I picked up the morning paper and saw a small notice on the bottom of the front page. Ken had died. His father died, just a short time later.

The prospect of life without the familiarity of his dad's care was unbearable. Death, to Ken, appeared to be more of a friend than the known hell of life. The irony is, life without his father was yet to be lived, and it didn't have to be hellish. I personally knew of people in his community who wanted to help him interpret the future as a friend. But Ken refused. What he knew of life appeared more ominous than what he knew of death.

When Is It Right to Die?
"When Death Is a Matter of Mercy."

Isaac Asimov once wrote, "No decent human being would allow an animal to suffer without putting it out of its misery. It is only to human beings that human beings are so cruel as to allow them to live on in pain, in hopelessness, in living death, without moving a muscle to help them."[5]

A long time ago, I went to see a movie with my friends called *They Shoot Horses, Don't They?* I had just been discharged from the rehab center, and my friends thought it would be nice to enjoy some Friday night fun. Besides, the title had "horses" in it, so the movie couldn't be that bad, right?

Wrong. It was a story about a depressed person who wanted a friend to put a gun to her head to relieve her suffering. When the friend protested, the character, played by Jane Fonda, said with woeful eyes, "They shoot horses, don't they?" At that point we left the movie.

Art sometimes imitates life, and although the message of that movie may have been shocking when it was released in 1969, today 67 percent of Americans and 38 percent of evangelical Christians approve, in certain cases, of mercy killing.[6]

But what induces a person to cause a death and say, "This is for your own good"? Is it indeed because pain is excessive? Pain management is the most sophisticated and advanced it's ever been. Is it the difficulty of living with limitations? Who knows what Arlene could have accomplished in the world of wheelchair sports if she had given her wheelchair half a chance. Is it a suffering loved one's shattered dignity and loss of hope? Are we motivated to mercy-kill because the loved one is hurting, or are we motivated by a confused sense of guilt and sympathy, suffering as we watch him or her? The key is, nobody (not even me) *wants* to be disabled. But once you experience that accident, once you are disabled, you may quickly change your mind about what makes life worth living. Life is *that* precious.

And no matter how forcibly Isaac Asimov or moviemakers may argue, animals aren't on the same level as humans. As Charles

Colson explains, "Humans are unique in all of creation: we are conscious of our existence, aware of death, capable of works of great creativity, and the only part of creation that bears the image of God. Humans alone have eternal souls, which confers unique moral status."[7] That's why putting down an injured horse is worlds away from killing a suffering person.

The dictionary defines *mercy* as "kind or compassionate treatment." And there are *much* better ways to demonstrate kindness and compassion than to send a loved one off into an irreversible death.

Defining the Right to Die

Just listen to a few people respond to the question "When is it right to die?" and you'll hear a mixed muddle of not only when, but who wants to die, how, and why! Of the people whose stories I shared above, no one was actually dying. Yet whether the person is dying, disabled, or terminally ill—or is the family member of one of these—all use similar language and arguments. To clear up the confusion, let's look at a few terms.

EUTHANASIA

Euthanasia is supposed to signify "good death," but today's meaning of the word is confusing because it conjures up images of everything from pulling the plug on a dying loved one to the killing of millions in Nazi Germany who were considered socially unuseful—useless eaters.

Practically speaking, euthanasia means to "bring about death" or "assist an individual in achieving death" because others, or even the patients themselves, consider their lives to be worthless. The motive is usually to relieve suffering, save money, or do away with the indignities associated with dying. Dr. C. Everett Koop, who served as US Surgeon General from 1982 to 1989, explained euthanasia this way:

> The whole thing about euthanasia comes down to one word: motive. If your motive is to alleviate suffering while a patient is going through the throes of dying, and you are using medication that alleviates suffering, even though it might shorten his life by a few hours, that is not euthanasia. But if you are giving him a drug intended to shorten his life, then your motivation is for euthanasia.[8]

In some cases, euthanasia has come to mean the deliberate act of causing the death of another person, commonly through lethal injection. There used to be a distinction between *active* euthanasia—mercy killing by which a person takes action to cause someone else's death—and *passive* euthanasia—mercy killing by withholding or withdrawing medical treatment or food and water. Now, however, all euthanasia is seen to be active, and the phrase "forgoing life-sustaining treatment" has taken the place of the term "passive euthanasia" in most cases.[9]

Voluntary euthanasia is to cause death with the person's approval and consent; *nonvoluntary euthanasia* is to cause death without a person's consent through approval secured from a family member, hospital panel, or court. The key is that the patient is incompetent, and someone else must decide either what the patient would have wanted or what is in his or her best interests.

Involuntary euthanasia is to cause the death of a person against his or her will under whatever circumstances. *Death selection* involves systematic involuntary euthanasia against the lives of people no longer considered socially useful. This type of euthanasia threatens a wide range of people, including the elderly, the habitually criminal, those who are mentally ill, and those with disabilities. Population control and cost containment are two primary arguments used when the subject is debated. Currently no groups are officially proposing death selection, but practically speaking, we see this happening with babies diagnosed with Down syndrome in the womb. Women who have this diagnosis confirmed through amniocentesis choose to abort their baby 90 percent of the time.

Assisted suicide is a term that describes a physician or family member aiding a person toward death. It can also be called medically assisted death or aid-in-dying.

DEATH WITH DIGNITY

Death with dignity is a phrase that tries to say one thing but ends up meaning another. After all, death is the final indignity of losing all that one possesses in life. Death remains, in the words of the apostle Paul in 1 Corinthians 15:26, "the last enemy." People may die serenely or peaceably, but with dignity? Modern usage of the phrase implies that death by suicide or homicide is inherently preferable to death by natural causes. Some say the dignity comes from the *choosing*, the being in control. Journalist Jason Barber writes, "Death with dignity is a human right: to retain control until the very end and, if the quality of your life is too poor, to decide to end your suffering; the dignity comes from exercising the choice."[10] Other euthanasia proponents explain that death with dignity means allowing a person to die free from the dehumanization and pain often brought about by the application of extraordinary medical efforts in the cold sterility of hospital wards.

Currently no laws require a dying person to be kept alive by heroic measures. Also, all mentally competent persons have the legal right to refuse medical treatment, provided they have received sufficient information from the physician to make an informed consent.[11] What's more, with an advance health care directive (discussed further in chapter 9), a person can make their wishes regarding medical treatment known before an accident or illness incapacitates them—and there are laws in many states that require doctors to abide by these directives.

RIGHT TO DIE

Right to die is another phrase that tries to say one thing but ends up meaning another. Taken literally, "right to die" is senseless. There's no such thing as a right to something unavoidable and inevitable. No one speaks of having a "right to jail time" after being convicted of a felony. But in common usage, the phrase sometimes means the "right to choose one's own kind of death" and at other times a supposed "right to be killed."

QUALITY OF LIFE

Quality of life is a phrase of recent phenomenon. A hundred years ago, people like me who broke their necks died—no need to worry about quality of life when you're dead.

Today it's a different story. Within the last several decades, medical technology has given us high-tech helps to improve a person's so-called quality of life. And this has granted society the power to control whether a person lives or dies, all depending on the application of a few technological marvels or complex drugs. For example, an air-pulse generator and inflatable vest used by my friend Veronica vibrates her airway walls in a therapy called high-frequency chest wall oscillation to counteract the effects of cystic fibrosis on her lungs. A sophisticated drug regimen stabilizes the moods of my neighbor Linda, who struggles with bipolar disorder. Or on a much simpler level, an indwelling catheter keeps the urinary plumbing of someone like me flowing.

Kidney machines, pacemakers, insulin injections, and medications to manage either pain or depression—all of these things, to one degree or another, increase one's "quality of life."

However, by virtue of these high-tech tools or drug therapies, people's lives begin to be defined by whether or not they can function. Don, thanks to a ventilator, is able to sit up in a wheelchair and go about life as a "normal" person. People like Lisa in pain or depression can, with medication, hold down a job and raise a family. They can function, and thus society moves them up a few notches on its quality-of-life scale, a few notches above others less able—such as my friends Paige and Tyson Snedeker, who were both born with a neuromuscular degenerative condition that has slowly taken their ability to move, see, hear, and even breathe on their own.

Some say a society that measures people in terms of quality of life will preserve those who have a potential to function . . . and will neglect those who don't. Oddly enough, society will ascribe to physically fit and intellectually capable people a very high quality of life, despite the fact that they are sometimes the most miserable, and a very low quality of life to people who are poor and disabled, despite the fact they are sometimes the most content. "Quality of life" is generally used as a counterbalance to the term *sanctity of life*. Which brings me to the next terms.

ABSOLUTE AND RELATIVE VALUE

Absolute value reflects the long-held ethic that human life holds complete worth without relationship to other factors, including a person's functioning ability. In other words, no matter how disabled Paige and Tyson become as a result of their degenerative condition, their lives will never lose value.

Relative value is what people ascribe to human life when it is appraised in relation to other factors, such as how much a person can or cannot do. By this definition, the value and meaning of Paige's or Tyson's life are related to how disabled they become.

From varying viewpoints, life has either absolute or relative value. Which is it? And how do those viewpoints have a bearing on preserving or rejecting the life of a warm-blooded, breathing human being like my friend Nancy Severns? Nancy has a connective tissue disorder, Lyme disease, and a host of other diagnoses that keep her in bed for all but a few minutes each day. She has been bedridden for nineteen months on account of pain and fatigue. Lying flat and faceup, she can't be too far above the bottom rung of society's quality-of-life ladder.

People's Viewpoints . . . Society's Trends

When? Who? What? How? Why? You know the issue is confusing when you have to get so nitpicky about definitions. And although dictionary terms make the life and death struggle sound neat and clean, it is not. Death is the great indignity, the last enemy, and we should be shocked by the stories of people like Arlene Randolph and Ken Bergstedt. But why aren't we?

Euthanasia is not uncommon. It has been closeted in hospital ethics committees as death certificates are divvied out, and cloaked in back rooms of maternity wards, where infants with severe disabilities have been left to starve to death.

On the one hand, it's good to yank euthanasia out into the open and expose it to public debate because people need to understand and be able to make informed decisions. On the other hand, the sheer repetition of stories like Arlene's and Ken's gradually dulls the shock effect. No longer is the public outraged by the starvation of infants born after botched abortions or the murder-suicides of caregivers solving the problem of their loved one's ongoing care through death. Instead, where there was once repulsion at the actions of the Dr. Kevorkian types, who made it possible for any despairing individual to orchestrate their own suicide, and revulsion at the methods for euthanasia involving the extremes of bullets, suffocation, or poisoning, much of the debate has now shifted to an acceptance of the premise of euthanasia but with differing opinions about the best means to achieve it.

In the last few decades, though no one can say exactly how it happened, the unthinkable became tolerable. And then acceptable. And then legal. And now, God help us, applaudable.

For centuries, civilized countries, through law and religion, safeguarded life, especially the lives of those who are weak and vulnerable. Increasingly, that is no longer the case. Instead, when a person who is disabled, elderly, or terminally ill wishes to end their life, it is considered courageous. When a person who is not in these categories wishes to do the same, it is considered suicide, and the individual receives treatment to help them overcome those desires. And what an irony that euthanasia has become popular at a time when our resources are boundlessly greater and our medical capabilities infinitely better than they were in the days when mercy killing was anathema.

But now, in the midst of greater resources and greater potential, we struggle to match our discussion of ethics with rapidly advancing medical technology. The passion to safeguard and exercise rights has resulted in sloppy definitions and unpardonable legislation. When it is no longer convenient to care for a person with disabilities, shouldn't the role of the state be to protect the weak and vulnerable and not to support their execution? It is the hallowed responsibility of government to safeguard the well-being of the weak and vulnerable, not to prematurely end their lives. Sadly, it has now become appropriate to kill a person because it's too hard and too emotionally distressing to keep them alive.

Influencers are proposing answers to the question of what is moral in relation to end-of-life decisions, and society, whether deliberately or unintentionally, is forming answers as well.

Now, what is your point of view?

Questions for Discussion and Reflection
Let's Define the Issues

People are defining the issues around the question "When is it right to die?" on a daily basis. A good working knowledge of the issues will help you be a better decision maker and also enable the church to speak to our society at large.

Consider the following answers to the question "When is it right to die?"

- "It's none of your business."
- "When it's too expensive to live."
- "When death is easier than facing life."
- "When death is a matter of mercy."

What would you say to those who give the above answers? Remember, these people aren't saying these things for the sake of academic discussion. They are in severe pain and/or despair.

Part Two

A TIME
TO CHOOSE

Chapter 4

YOUR DECISION
MATTERS TO OTHERS

No man is an island entire of itself; every man is a piece
of the continent, a part of the main . . . Any man's death
diminishes me, because I am involved in mankind; and
therefore never send to know for whom the bell tolls;
it tolls for thee.

JOHN DONNE

For the moment, forget everything you've ever heard about right-to-die or right-to-life positions. Put aside the court rulings. Push out of your mind the tug-at-your-heart stories you've seen in the movies or read about online.

Now, with no one reading your thoughts, may I ask, "Do you know when it is right to die? For you? For your family?" Please, I realize this may not be a theoretical question for you. You may be one who could write a real-life tug-at-your-heart story. And you may have already made up your mind about how and when you want to die. Whatever your response, I want you to know that your decision matters.

It matters more than you realize.

Let me explain. Since at one time I served on a national council that drafted major civil rights legislation, my husband, Ken, then a high school government teacher, asked me to speak to his classes on the subject of legalizing euthanasia. This was well before California had legalized medically assisted death, but plenty of initiatives were testing the waters. Ken wanted me to talk to his students about the implications of a right-to-die law. The classroom was crowded with kids standing along the back and leaning against the chalkboards covering the walls.

I was surprised by how interested they were as I divulged my despair of earlier days. I admitted my relief that no right-to-die law existed when I was in the hospital and hooked up to machines. I then underscored how critical it was for every student to become informed and involved in shaping society's response to the problem. Then I added, "What role do you think society should play in helping people decide when it is right to die?"

A few hands went up. I could tell by their answers that they felt society should take action to help hurting and dying people—some students insisting on life no matter how burdensome the treatment, and a few wanting to help by hurrying along the death process.

One student shared how his mother was getting demoralized by the burden of taking care of his sister with developmental delays. He felt society should, in his words, "do something."

"Like what?" I playfully challenged.

"Like . . . I'm not sure, but society ought to get more involved in the lives of people like my mother."

I glanced at Ken. He nodded, as if to give the go-ahead to take a free rein with this young man. "May I ask what you have done to get more involved?"

The student smiled and shrugged.

"How have you helped alleviate the burden? Have you taken your sister on an outing lately? Maybe to the beach?" I teased. "Have you offered to do some shopping for your mother? Maybe your mom wouldn't be so demoralized, maybe she wouldn't feel so stressed or burdened, if you rolled up your sleeves a little higher to help."

A couple of his friends by the chalkboard laughed and threw wads of paper at him. "Okay, okay, I see your point," he chuckled.

I smiled. "My point is this: Society is not a bunch of people way out there who sit around big tables and think up political trends or cultural drifts; society is you. Your actions, your decisions, matter. What you do or don't do has a ripple effect on everyone around you. And on a smaller scale, your participation can even make a huge difference in what your family decides to do with your sister."

The classroom fell silent, and I knew the lesson was being driven home. I paused, scanned the face of each student, and closed by saying, "You, my friends, are society."

Your Point of View Matters

And that's how much your point of view matters. You may be the one who fiercely advocates pulling the plug, or the one who fights to keep a heart pumping until the bitter end. Whichever it is, you must, in the words of John Donne, know this: no man is an island.

We are such private people. We would like to be able to make a life or death decision in a vacuum or even at an arm's-length distance from others. But we can't. Your point of view and how you act on it, let's say as you lie in bed with a terminal illness, not only matters to you and your family; it matters to a wide network of friends and associates as well. In other words, to society. The cultural drift is channeled by your decision to either pull the plug or hold on to life.

In fact, will you permit me to get personal? If you can, dismiss your real-life circumstances for a moment. Let's pretend you *are* in bed with a terminal illness, and doctors say you could live for another six months. Your pain can be effectively managed. And you have an opportunity to make a choice about medical treatment. You can decline treatment if you want—and you even live in a state whose laws permit you to request a medically assisted death. Your family says it's up to you. I know it's hard to pretend such an antiseptic situation, devoid of real grief and actual anguish, because distress would play a key role. But given this sterile scenario, what would you do? What would you say?

Are you one who might say, "It's none of your business. I'll control how and when I die, and what's more, I feel no responsibility to society. I'm only responsible to myself and to those I love."

I hear what you're saying. But when people maintain that their death is their own business and the business of "those I love," they do not consider the significance of their decision on the wider circle of life. A decision to cut life short, even if only a few months, does not stop with "those I love," but affects a whole network of relationships: friends, former colleagues, teachers, distant family members, casual acquaintances, and even nurses and doctors who occasionally stop by your bedside.

Just what effect might your decision have? Your gutsy choice to face suffering head-on forces others around you to sit up and take notice. It's called strengthening the character of a helping society. When people observe perseverance, endurance, and courage, their moral fiber is reinforced. Conversely, your choice to bow out of life can and does weaken the moral resolve of that same society.

Years after my hospitalization, my mother continued to receive letters from nurses, cafeteria workers, and a family whose daughter had suffered a severe brain injury and had been hooked up to machines two beds away from me in the intensive care unit. My parents made gutsy choices that involved facing suffering head-on. And the decisions they made regarding my care had a lasting impact on these people. And who knows what ripple effects have come from the choices *they* have made in the years since?

If you believe your decision is private and independent, think again. Your choice to speed up the dying process is like playing a delicate game of pick-up sticks. You carefully lift a stick, hoping not to disturb the intricate web. But just when you think you've succeeded, your independent action ends up jiggling the fragile balance and sending other sticks rolling.

And as the apostle Paul writes in Romans 14:7, "None of us lives for ourselves alone, and none of us dies for ourselves alone."

You Have Your Rights . . . Sort Of

"But I have a right to decide what's best for me," you may say. "I'm entitled to exercise my independence. It's fundamental to what this country is all about. Even the courts recognize my autonomy as a patient."

True, because you are a mentally competent person, the judge would probably bang the gavel in your favor. Like you said, you have rights, and you may end up literally dying for them.

But like all other liberties, your choice is not absolute—no ifs, ands, or buts. Your self-determination to die has strings attached if it adversely affects the rights of others. That's why more than half the states in our country have laws against aiding a person in suicide. Even states that have legalized physician-assisted suicide still have laws against just anyone assisting. And also, these laws insist—though not always followed in practice—that the patient be in the final six months of a terminal illness and be able to make the final action that brings about their death. Why all the legal safeguards? Think it through: if everybody ended their life as a solution to problems, the very fabric of our society would ultimately unravel, and with it all the other individual rights we enjoy.

Yes, you have a glistening right of privacy, as long as it does not overshadow the rights of others. But legalized euthanasia can seriously infringe on the rights of many physicians. You might want to exercise a right to die, but do you have the right to ask a physician, whose duty is to heal, to comply with your wishes or even to make a referral? No person, in the name of self-determination, should be able to oblige a doctor to prescribe a fatal dose when it goes against the physician's oath to "do no harm." Yet already we have seen lawsuits against doctors who refuse to assist in hastening a patient's death. Or again, in death with dignity acts, there is no requirement that next of kin be notified before a person follows through on his or her plan to hasten death. Shouldn't parents, a spouse, or children have the right to know before their loved one is beyond their reach?

But wait, it sounds a little like we're trading baseball cards here. Like, "My rights are more valuable than yours!"

"Oh, yeah? Well, my one right is worth more than your three combined!"

Our rights are not things that can be exchanged, bargained over, or transferred like property. Essentially, rights are *moral claims* to be recognized by law, not things to be traded.[1] And moral claims have to take into account responsibility, limits on freedom, and ethical standards that reflect the good of the entire community.

When we clamor about the sanctity of our individual rights, we may be reinforcing an all-too-human failing, namely, the tendency to place ourselves at the center of the moral universe. If taken to the extreme, clamor over individual rights can lead to one indignation after another about the inherent limitations of society, and we will never be satisfied.

The fact is, true rights are based in God's moral law. Proverbs 31:8–9 reads, "Speak up for those who cannot speak for themselves, for the rights of all who are destitute. Speak up and judge fairly; defend the rights of the poor and needy." But take God out of the picture, and rights become nothing more than people's willful determinations dressed up in the language of "rights" to give them a showy kind of dignity. Then the exercise of rights becomes nothing more than a national competition between who is more victimized than whom.

As I shared in my husband's government class, "You, my friend, are society." So welcome to the club of community, and even though some may try to drown out other styles of discourse with shouts about personal rights, the community may have a thing or two to say, and it may say it a lot louder. After all, community can only progress when its individuals exercise higher moral choices, and community is sacrificed when individuals choose with only themselves in mind.

Legalized Euthanasia: A Good Law for a Better Society?

When I first wrote *When Is It Right to Die?* legalization of assisted suicide had not yet come to any modern country. Now that laws such as Oregon's Death with Dignity Act have been on the books for two decades, we have the ability to reflect on the reasons patients have chosen to end their lives. When prescribing doctors fill out a final report after an assisted suicide, the top four reasons given for the request for assisted suicide are these:

- decreasing ability to participate in activities that made life enjoyable (96.2 percent)
- loss of autonomy (92.4 percent)
- loss of dignity (75.4 percent)
- a sense of being a burden (48.1 percent)[2]

These have nothing to do with pain from a terminal disease. Rather, these are psychological issues that can be effectively treated. Yet these laws do not even require that psychological support services be provided to alleviate these problems. All too often, when the medical condition is fraught with challenges, people—even doctors—tend to think, *You're better off dead than disabled.*

Like in the story of Brittany Maynard. When Brittany, a twenty-nine-year-old woman, was diagnosed with a glioblastoma brain tumor and given only six months to live, she felt she could not face the pain and humiliation of a difficult death. She moved from her home in California to Oregon so she could take her own life under Oregon's Death with Dignity Act. Brittany spoke of her choice as a highly personal and private one, but it was not. During her very public last few months, her journey was broadcast through her own personal Facebook page and through interviews and articles in major news outlets. She campaigned extensively to have medically assisted suicide legalized in her home state, and shortly after her death in November 2014, California passed the End of Life Option Act. This act was touted as giving people choice and control at the end of life. Yet experience with euthanasia laws elsewhere proves otherwise.

So what has happened in the twenty years since physician-assisted suicide became legal in the United States? What has happened since countries like Belgium took a strong stance for euthanasia?

Legalized euthanasia results in physicians being cast in the role of killer, not healer. For some twenty-four hundred years, people who are terminally ill, dying, or disabled have had the assurance that doctors operate under the Hippocratic Oath, an oath to heal them, not kill them. But fewer and fewer medical schools consider this classic oath relevant. The oath used by Loma Linda University School of Medicine, for instance—a school committed to "training skilled medical professionals with a commitment to Christian service"—lists no objections to abortion and euthanasia, as contained in the original Hippocratic Oath.[3] Other medical schools now allow students to draft their own oaths to reflect whatever modern values they wish to uphold.

To change the oath is one thing, but to say "role of killer"? Isn't that a little much? Scott and Sheryl Crosier's experience in Missouri suggests otherwise. Their son Simon was born with Trisomy 18 and apnea. Only after Simon was denied resuscitation and died did they learn that Simon's pediatrician had placed a DNR (Do Not Resuscitate) in his file.[4] A survey of neonatal-perinatal pediatricians found that 25 percent would feel it permissible to place a DNAR (Do Not Attempt Resuscitation) in a patient's file *without a parent's consent*, based on long-term prospects for poor quality of life. I find it no surprise that doctors who have joined the medical field within the last fifteen years are more comfortable issuing such a DNAR than doctors with more than fifteen years of experience.[5]

In Belgium, during the year 2013, doctors intentionally killed approximately one thousand people without their consent. While the law there requires doctors to report the deaths they facilitate, there have been no penalties for doctors who openly admit to killing more patients than they report.[6]

Legalized euthanasia results in less care for the dying. Barbara Wagner's lung cancer had come back. She had fought it off once before with her insurance through Oregon's health plan, but the treatment her doctor prescribed this time was different. And expensive—$4,000 a month. It was hard enough to process the grim news the cancer was back, and then Barbara got the letter from the state's health plan. The treatment wasn't covered, but it *would* cover the drugs necessary for a physician-assisted death. After all, those drugs only cost about $50.[7]

What about that is a dignified death? Rather than allowing doctors to provide better care, legalized euthanasia gives permission to suggest to hurting individuals that society is eager to see their death. It's a matter of economics. Euthanasia is extraordinarily cheap when compared to the costs of humane chronic and terminal care.

Legalized euthanasia establishes a fundamental right to die. Even with supposed safeguards written into physician-assisted suicide legislation, these laws are stacked against the patient and apply to people with years, even decades, to live. Doctors make the determination that a person is terminally ill, and doctors are often wrong in predicting life expectancy. Brittany Maynard took her fatal dose a full month after the six months her doctors predicted she had remaining. During her last week and a half of life, she still felt well enough to travel from her home to visit the Grand Canyon. How much longer might she have lived, how many other moments of beauty could she have experienced, if she had not taken her own life?

Ms. Maynard is not alone in this. In the official language of Oregon's Death with Dignity Act, doctors must believe a person has only six months left to live before the person is eligible for medical aid-in-dying. Of the 859 individuals who died from ingesting a lethal prescription in Oregon during the years 1998–2014, some patients lived *more than two and a half years* after first requesting a fatal dose.[8]

And about that definition of terminal illness . . . an eighteen-year-old with insulin-dependent diabetes is eligible for assisted suicide. Why? The definition includes any condition that would be fatal without treatment. Without insulin injections, a teen's life expectancy with Type 1 diabetes is frightfully brief. But insulin pumps and blood sugar monitoring have become so much easier to use in recent years, and now the life expectancy of an insulin-dependent person is age sixty-six for men and sixty-eight for women.[9] Yet legalized aid-in-dying measures, as written in California and Oregon, make it possible for an eighteen-year-old, perhaps depressed by a recent diagnosis or even a breakup, to request—and receive—medical assistance for committing suicide.

The United States Constitution affirms that fundamental rights cannot be limited to any one group, such as the terminally ill. While we may soon see a trend of nonterminally ill people—clinically depressed persons, children with cystic fibrosis, nursing home residents, people with HIV/AIDS, and those who want to avoid large medical bills—demanding equal rights access to medically assisted suicide, already the "right" has been extended to some of these individuals without any action from the courts.

Michael Freeland struggled with depression since his mother's suicide when he was a young man. Over the next forty years, Michael's community and medical care team worked together to help him overcome the suicidal thoughts that would hit him. The legalization of physician-assisted suicide changed that. Shortly after he was diagnosed with lung cancer, he again expressed his desire to "end it all." This time, though, he called the politically active group Compassion in Dying Federation, which shepherds more than 75 percent of assisted suicides in the state of Oregon. And Michael, known for his long history of suicidal thoughts, received a prescription for fatal drugs without any mental health evaluation. Over the next months and years, he received, on the one hand, cancer treatment, pain management, social services, counseling, and in-home care and, on the other hand, disinterested prompting and coaching to follow through with his suicidal thoughts.[10] How is that compassion in dying?

Legalized euthanasia reveals that the character of a helping society is beginning to disintegrate. Marc and Eddy Verbessem had lived their entire lives together. Forty-six-year-old twins, they shared an apartment and a career as cobblers in Belgium. They also shared deafness and approaching blindness. The encroaching physical darkness seemed too much to bear, and Belgium is one of a handful of countries where nonterminally ill individuals can openly request, and be granted, assistance in dying. So these brothers sought out a doctor who would give them both lethal injections.[11] Sadly, this doctor found it far easier to kill than to cure, or even care. What might have happened if Marc and Eddy had received a different kind of help? Could their story have rivaled the success stories that come out of the Helen Keller National Center for Deaf-Blind Youths and Adults?[12]

Around the world, people with disabilities are reporting acts of disablism—harmful discrimination against people with disabilities and outright attacks. Society assigns no positive value to suffering and is becoming more and more oriented toward a culture of comfort. Without apology, people with disabilities have been told, "I'd rather die than be disabled like you."[13] People in need of financial assistance because of a disability have been called out through hate speech suggesting that such individuals are a "threat to the republic" and lazy.[14] Even more disheartening, violent crimes against persons with disability are at least twice the number of crimes against persons without disability.[15]

Legalized euthanasia broadens the "right to die" to a right to be killed. In the fall of 2015, forty-six-year-old Chris Dunn was hospitalized due to a mass on his pancreas. Sadly, there was nothing the hospital's medical team could do to cure him. But that was not the end of the nightmare for Chris and his loved ones. The hospital staff told his mother they wanted to turn off his life support *and* administer a drug that would end Chris's life in three to five minutes.[16] This was not a case of concerned individuals arguing about what the patient would have wanted. Chris was *fully conscious* and able to communicate his desires—and he wanted to live.[17] Texas law allows health care providers to remove life-sustaining treatment from a patient, even when doing so overrides the patient's desire and right to live. Chris's family took the issue to the courts, but Chris died of natural causes before a decision could be reached. How could this happen? Chris was uninsured. The economic burden of his care seemed to justify his murder.

And what of other vulnerable people, such as those who are poor or senile?

Kate Cheney began showing signs of dementia. It wasn't surprising, as she had reached the ripe old age of eighty-five. She then was diagnosed with terminal cancer. Her personal physician refused to write her a prescription for a lethal dose. A psychiatrist concluded that Kate wasn't even asking for one; it seemed her daughter was the one pushing for it. Finally, a prescribing physician agreed to write Kate the prescription. A month went by, and then her daughter needed a break from caregiving, so Kate spent a week in a nursing home. The night she returned home, with the help of her daughter and family, she swallowed the prescription drugs that killed her.[18]

Can we even know what Kate's mental state was the night of her death? The only witnesses to her death were the same family members suspected to have coached her through her request for the lethal prescription. Even aside from the concern of lucidity and the question of who really wanted this option, could she simply have been depressed after a week in the care of strangers, only to return home to the sad truth that her daughter was not up to the task of caring for her long term?

Perhaps you think these are just isolated incidences, mere bureaucratic mistakes. No one intends for this blatant disregard for a person's right to life to happen. The laws spelling out physician-assisted suicide just apply to those who are terminally ill and *want* to hasten death.

Not necessarily. I'm not being an alarmist. Just look at Nancy Fitzmaurice, a twelve-year-old girl with significant disabilities in the United Kingdom whose mother successfully petitioned the judge to allow her to starve to death, even though at the time of the judge's ruling, UK laws prohibited assisted suicide.[19] Many states in the US prohibit parental access to the health records of twelve-year-old children, citing the adolescent's right to privacy and autonomy regarding health care decisions. Yet for Nancy, it was just *assumed* she would want death hastened.

Would we dare assume the same of Carol Walters?

Dear Joni,

My name is Carol Walters. I was born with cerebral palsy. I walk with a limp, and I can use my hands, but I have poor control.

I was thinking how I don't think a person with a disability should take his or her life any more than anyone else should. I feel we are here to live our lives to contribute to our place where we live. Everyone has something to offer.

I have a part-time job at city hall in my town. At work I am known as Smiley. I clean up the community building, and I sweep walks. I feel God has put me at that job for a reason. I think that reason is to help people realize I can live a full and happy life the way I am.

I do have moments feeling sorry for myself, and there are times I wish God would make me normal. I talk to my mom, and she helps me see that I have many blessings.

Love,

Carol Walters

Questions for Discussion and Reflection
No Man Is an Island

Helen is a forty-three-year-old woman with cancer. Though her cancer was relatively mild for some time, her condition has rapidly worsened. She has had several bouts of depression. Her three kids have handled the situation surprisingly well, but it is beginning to wear on them and on her husband. She has gone through several kinds of treatments. The latest report from the doctor indicated she is a candidate for a bone-marrow transplant. Helen does not want to have the transplant done.

1. Who would be affected by Helen's decision in this scenario? Are there others who would be affected by her decision who are not referred to in the scenario?

2. If Helen did not have the transplant, what impact would it have on the family? How do you think each would respond?

3. Helen is a devoted mother. It's hard to think she wouldn't consider the impact on her family. Assuming she has thought about the impact, what conclusions do you think she came to that led her to believe that trying the transplant was not worth it? Here are some examples:

   - "My family needs to get on with their life. This is depressing them, and my marriage could fall apart."
   - "We can't afford the surgery. College bills are coming in just a few years."
   - "I'll take my chances without the transplant."

Given Helen's reasons, do you agree or disagree with her?

Chapter 5

YOUR DECISION MATTERS TO YOU

Wherever the providence of God may dump us down, in a slum, in a shop, in the desert, we have to labour along the line of His direction. Never allow this thought—"I am of no use where I am," because you certainly can be of no use where you are not! Wherever He has engineered your circumstances, pray.

OSWALD CHAMBERS

We are now at the part where I wish there were no pages between us. I'd love to be able to wheel up to you as you sit at your daughter's hospital bedside, past the beeping machines and dripping tubing, to talk face-to-face. Or be with you at your kitchen table to hear your heartache over your senile mother in a nursing home. Or just sit and listen as you lift the black cloak of depression long enough to speak.

If we were together, I'd want to talk about facing suffering:

the kind that spins out of control, rips into your sanity, and tears apart your body—the kind of suffering that helpful information is powerless against.

If we were together, I'd want to peel back our defenses and confess how we both would really rather sidestep the whole process of pain. How we'd like to detour the distress and shortcut the suffering. Sure, we can say life is not something to be discarded when it doesn't work properly or seem to have value, but it is a constant struggle to hold on to it. How much easier to bypass it all.

For several years leading up to my diagnosis of stage 3 cancer, I wrestled with chronic pain. The pain opened a frightening door to depression, and I found myself saying, "God, I can't imagine living the rest of my life in this much pain." At several points, I almost hoped I'd be diagnosed with some terminal condition—perhaps cancer—so I could escape my ensuing years of pain. Could cancer be, I wondered, my early ticket to heaven? Sure enough, the very day in June 2010 that I learned I had cancer, my depression disappeared overnight. I thought my earthly graduation to heaven wouldn't be far away. But God had other plans, and I am so glad He did.

Sidestepping the Process of Pain

No thinking person chooses suffering. But we can choose our attitude in the midst of suffering.

That lesson was driven home to me years ago when I read *Man's Search for Meaning*, a classic study of how people preserve their spiritual freedom and exhibit heroic responses in the face of horrible suffering. The author, Viktor Frankl, was a psychiatrist who was sent to a concentration camp in World War II, where he found himself stripped to naked existence, cold, starved, beaten,

and expecting extermination with each passing day. He lost his
friends and family to the gas ovens. He lost every valued possession.
How could he find life worth preserving?

The book hit home with me as a young student, even though
campus life was far from the terrors of Auschwitz. But Viktor
Frankl's work meant far more to me during the darkest, loneliest
days of my two-year confinement in the hospital. There, lying
facedown, strapped on a Stryker frame, I turned each page of
Man's Search for Meaning with a mouthstick clutched between my
teeth. My tears would drop and splatter on pages where this camp
survivor wrote:

> We who lived in concentration camps can remember
> the men who walked through the huts comforting others,
> giving away their last piece of bread. They may have been
> few in number, but they offer sufficient proof that every-
> thing can be taken from a man but one thing: the last of the
> human freedoms—to choose one's attitude in any given set
> of circumstances, to choose one's own way.
>
> And there were always choices to make. Every day, every
> hour, offered the opportunity to make a decision, a decision
> which determined whether you would or would not submit to
> those powers which threatened to rob you of your very self,
> your inner freedom; which determined whether or not you
> would become the plaything of circumstance.[1]

This man was worlds apart from my vocational rehab counselor. Frankl had experienced great suffering, and so *his* words
commanded my attention. I remember pausing to give my mouth
a break from page turning, murmuring over and over, "I am *not*
held hostage by my disability . . . I am *not* held hostage by my

disability." Mine was not so much a spiritual exercise as a mental effort, a first-step attempt at breaking free of the circumstances that dug their claws of control into me. I would read on:

> Even though conditions such as lack of sleep, insufficient food and various mental stresses may suggest that the inmates were bound to react in certain ways, in the final analysis it becomes clear that the sort of person the prisoner became was the result of an *inner decision*, and not the result of camp influences alone . . . When we are no longer able to change a situation—just think of an incurable disease such as inoperable cancer—we are challenged to change ourselves.[2]

I was challenged to change myself. But how? I felt a little sheepish that my inner decision could barely move me to smile in my wheelchair, let alone face with courage things like starvation, beatings, and gas ovens.

When I finished Frankl's book, I realized it was an answer to one basic question, a question that in fact the psychiatrist, after he was released and returned to his practice, often asked his troubled patients: "Why do you *not* commit suicide?"

In other words, "Why do you *not* sidestep suffering?"

From their answers, it was then the goal of the psychiatrist to weave these slender threads of broken lives into a pattern of meaning. Each person, he insisted, could find valuable meaning in suffering.

I mused over the meaning of my suffering while lying right side up on my Stryker frame rather than upside down—it was easier to think hopeful thoughts facing fresh air rather than the floor! As I counted the tiles on the ceiling, I counted the few, slender, brightly shining threads of my broken life.

- I'm alive.
- I at least still have feeling in my neck and tops of my shoulders.
- I can see the moon through my hospital window.
- I'm learning that patience and endurance mean more on a Stryker frame than running twenty-five laps around a soccer field.
- My friends are still coming to see me, and the doughnuts they bring taste good.
- It's nice to have the nurse read me Robert Frost's poetry during her lunch break.
- I like listening to the Beatles.
- And like holding on to a thin kite string, I have hope that my situation might get better. I see it in the eyes and smiles of my family, my friends, and a few of the nurses.
- Oh, and one more positive thing—they might find a cure for spinal cord injury!

Small as they were, these slender threads tied me to life, even if I hadn't yet decided if it was worth living. The threads were fragile, but they held me through the day and kept me connected to people. The meaning behind it all, however, was still unclear. But I knew this much: it had something to do with God.

Someone has said if you believe that the individual is supreme, then your responsibility is only to yourself since there is no God who gives us life or who awaits us in death. But if you believe that life derives from a loving Creator, then leapfrogging the suffering process must be considered within a larger context.[3]

It was a fact that my background oriented me toward God. And my assessment about life and death was becoming a matter of conscience rather than a knee-jerk reaction to the problems at hand. The weeks passed. My thoughts deepened. And the longer I hung in there through the process of suffering, the stronger the weave became in the fabric of meaning. I was convinced God was mysteriously behind the pattern, so I took a closer look at new threads.

- My friendships are deepening and becoming more honest.
- What's important in life are people.
- I'm learning the value of a smile.
- God is real. I can feel Him when I'm alone at night.
- There are others who are hurting a lot more than me, and I'm beginning to care, honestly care, about them.

What were once slender threads were now becoming cords. And the fabric of meaning behind my suffering was beginning to take shape. Life, I was discovering, was worth living.

Is Weaving the Threads Worth the Effort?

That's all well and good for me. And it's all well and good for Viktor Frankl. But a quadriplegic and a death camp survivor can't simply paste the threads of our experiences on others who want to sidestep their suffering. What about someone like Larry McAfee, a civil engineer who was paralyzed from the neck down in a motorcycle accident and whose life was being sustained on a ventilator?

Unable to move out of a nursing home and unable to breathe on his own, Larry asked the courts to allow him to pull the plug on his ventilator and die. The court petition simply stated that Larry "has no control over his person and receives no enjoyment out of life."[4]

I wasted no time in writing Larry.

Dear Larry,

Like you, I've experienced being reduced to just existing—
the basics of breathing, eating, and sleeping. Lying there,
I felt as though my experience represented every human (it's
just that the rest of the human race didn't realize they were
merely breathing and sleeping—they were too busy being on
their feet with a lot of distractions). After much thinking,
I realized that there *had* to be more to life for everybody than
just mere existence. And if not, then why not everybody "pull
the plug," no matter if they were disabled or not!

In a way, I felt as though Viktor Frankl were looking over my
shoulder from his bunk bed in that concentration camp. He would
agree that there had to be more to life than just existing, going through
the motions, getting born and then growing old and then dying. But
I wanted to take it a step further from the advice of the psychiatrist;
I wanted to talk to Larry about God.[5] I continued my letter:

At that point, I came to the conclusion that there had to
be a personal God who cared for me and everybody else if,
indeed, life was to make sense. There must be a God . . . and
if not, then the whole human race should put a gun to its head
if it wants to. But humans are too unique, too significant
to just put ourselves out of our misery if we can't handle
suffering. No, there must be a God who cares. There must be.

As I wrote, I wished there were no pages between Larry and
me. I would have given anything to wheel into his room and angle
my chair close to his bed so he could see me through the tubes and
machines. If we were together, I'd confess how I, too, at one time
wanted to sidestep the process of pain.

And I would tell Larry that God knew exactly how we both felt. God wasn't holed up in an ivory tower in the corner of the universe. He suffered too. Even Jesus was tempted to give in. He even sought, if possible, to avoid the suffering of the cross, pleading, "Father, if you are willing, take this cup from me." In Gethsemane as the shadow of His death approached, Jesus felt alone and distressed with no one around who could understand. So He turned to His Father, the only one He could talk to: "And being in anguish, he prayed more earnestly."[6]

And then, if I could have been sitting next to Larry, I would have told him that Jesus' decision to face the cross squarely secured a deeper meaning for the suffering of us all—more meaning than we could possibly imagine.

As I dropped my letter to Larry into the mailbox, I hoped he would find his own few brightly shining threads of meaning. But virtually the next day, I saw the headline: "Judge Rules Quadriplegic Entitled to End Own Life." My shoulders slumped when I also read that the judge said, "The ventilator to which he is attached is not prolonging his life; it is prolonging his death." A petition included an affidavit stating, "'I understand turning off the ventilator will result in my death,' signed by a shaky 'X' made with a pencil held in McAfee's mouth."[7]

That made me, an activist and advocate, steaming mad! If that judge had been approached by a poor minority woman who could no longer endure racism, sexism, and poverty, and she wanted aid to end her life painlessly, the woman would have been refused flat-out. In fact, she would be offered support in seeking better housing and a job—and well she should! But when a person with disabilities like Larry McAfee declares the same intention, people assume death is his best option.

Back to Larry's story. What happened next was a little confusing.

For some reason, he decided not to have himself removed from the ventilator. Next, Larry was transferred from the nursing home to another facility. His story dropped out of the papers, and I was unable to hunt up his new address. I had no idea where Larry was or what he was thinking, but I kept pulling for him from a distance, praying he would find those threads of meaning for his life.

Finally, after several years, I tracked him down. I was itching to find out why he decided to live, so I called him up. We chatted for a few moments, talking about quadriplegia and pressure sores, and then I got a little more serious. "Larry," I asked, "why did you decide not to follow through on assisted suicide? What was your reason to keep on living?"

He managed to speak between huffs and puffs of his ventilator. "Because I'm not forced to live in an institution or hospital anymore. I'm living in a little independent-living house with two other guys in wheelchairs. It's a lot more enjoyable with a lot less pressure, less rigid. You can set your own schedule. As long as I'm not forced to live under the conditions of the state, then I consider life worth living."

My eyes lit up. I inhaled deeply and then exhaled slowly. He was right. Too many severely disabled people feel trapped, even warehoused in institutions. Saving people's lives and rehabilitating them are pointless goals if they are denied the right and the means to control their lives. I prodded him a bit more. "So it's a chance to forge friendships, pursue hobbies?"

"Yeah, just to feel more human."

"What was it like in the institution?"

Larry paused a moment. "I just existed from day to day. But here I'm able to meet people on an equal basis."

This man sounded like he found his brightly shining threads. Slender, just a few of them, but threads strong enough to weave meaning into his life. As I listened, I kept whispering thanks under my breath. As John Donne poignantly wrote, "Any man's death diminishes me," and Larry's death would have diminished me, especially me, another quadriplegic![8]

I dared one more question. "Any advice you can give to people who, like you and me, can't use their hands or legs, maybe they're in wheelchairs?"

The line went quiet, and I could tell he was thinking. "I'll be honest. If a person, after years of trying, feels like he can't go on, then I feel it's within his right to . . . well, you know."

My spirits sagged a little. But I was thankful that he, at least, felt like he *could* go on. And I took comfort from the fact that his decision to live had most assuredly inspired others to do the same. Just then Larry added, "But I'd tell them, 'Don't rush into any hasty decisions, but give things a lot of thought and time. Don't try to conform to society. Give it time. Seek some guidance, not only from God, but from friends and family too.'"

Friends.

Family.

God.

These were the brightly shining threads in his life. Warm, caring, available people who accepted him, brought him out of social isolation, listened to his anger, helped him discover truths about himself, and encouraged him to interpret his future as a friend.[9]

They were people who circumvented the crippling health care system that had sentenced him to an institution and denied him the self-determination to live independently. They were people who put together the concept of the little independent-living center, who recognized Larry's freedom to set his own schedule and live as he wished. They were people who became his friends at the center and, from what he said at the close of our phone conversation, perhaps even helped him find God.

Larry learned what every hurting person who chooses life discovers: *answers most often come in the form of people rather than legal rulings.*

Helpful Information *and . . .*

People. I don't think Larry would have made it without them. His was a burden that needed bearing. His misery needed mercy. He didn't need an argument, a rational discussion, or placement in a suicide-prevention program. What he needed was a few people ready to give practical love, the kind of love that has its sleeves rolled up. And Larry's friends weren't the type to point him to an inspirational internet meme with a fancy font. They helped him to live, love, fight, breathe, and make his life his own.

Men and women said to Larry, "Choose life."

Friends said to me, "Believe in God."

Even Viktor Frankl said to thousands in despair, "Suffering can have meaning."

And thankfully, these people did not wad up truths into clichés and platitudes to be tossed at us who hurt, while they stood at a distance. "Believe in God" glowed with the warm heartbeat of love that was as real as flesh and blood. "Choose life" were words spoken straight ahead with a smile that included, that invited. "Suffering can have meaning" was the comfort that gently enfolded.

Helpful information is not enough. No one comes out of despair alive without a caring friend on the other side. For, as Ecclesiastes 4:9–10 reads, "two are better than one, because they have a good return for their labor: If either of them falls down, one can help the other up. But pity anyone who falls and has no one to help them up."

You cannot, you *must* not, suffer alone. It matters to the point of life and death.

Questions for Discussion and Reflection
It's about You

You've spent time deciding on other people's scenarios. Now it's time to write your own. About you! Choose an issue—death, health, or disability—and make up a scenario with some pertinent details.

Now answer the following questions and share them with the group.

1. What impact will the medical crisis you've described have on you? Be honest. You know how you've responded to crises in the past. Use that experience to picture what would happen to you:
   - emotionally
   - in your relationship with other people
   - in your relationship with God
2. What good do you think could come out of your situation?
3. How might you grow in your relationship with God?
4. What might you pray in the midst of your issue?

Chapter 6

YOUR DECISION MATTERS TO THE ENEMY

If we cannot be torn in pieces by the roaring lion, we may be hugged to death by the bear. The devil cares very little which it is, as long as he destroys our love for Christ and our confidence in Him.

CHARLES SPURGEON

I'll never forget the first day of my marriage to Ken. What a carefree, delightful morning!

As our jet lifted off from Los Angeles to fly us to our honeymoon in Hawaii, we cuddled and kissed. The flight attendants giggled and presented us with a cake and a couple of leis. After they served refreshments, we settled back and put on the earphones to watch the in-flight movie. To my surprise, it was *Whose Life Is It Anyway?*—a film about a quadriplegic who tried to get everyone, from his friends to his doctor to his lawyer, to give him the right to die.

Ken and I pulled off our earphones. This was not the time to think about the depression of quadriplegia or the desire it often brings to cut one's life short.

As the opening credits appeared on the screen, the flight attendant knelt by my seat and whispered, "Oh, Mrs. Tada, I'm very sorry about the movie selection today. Shall we change your seat?"

I smiled and shook my head no. I knew I had hope and a future, although I had a difficult time for the rest of the flight convincing the attendants that I was not bothered by the visual images on the screen. Yet even as Ken and I snuggled and talked of our future, I kept sneaking peeks at the film.

Without the soundtrack, strange and twisted thoughts began to whisper and wheedle into my brain. *Does Ken really know what he's gotten himself into? What if we can't handle it? Divorce and suicide happen to couples like us all the time. What if . . .*

Hold it! This was the happiest day of my life, and I refused to entertain such deplorable thoughts. I shook my head, jerked my attention away from the movie, and riveted it totally on Ken. I wasn't about to allow subtle ideas, like flying birds, to build a nest in my head.

It's called resisting temptation.

A provoking thought. A strong inclination. An inducement, an enticement to give in and give up. A crazy idea that settles in and begins to sound pleasing and plausible.

Thoughts leading to death begin that way.

I've had enough experience with temptation to know that such provocations aren't furtive ideas that dart out of nowhere, disjointed and having no connection. There exists an intelligence behind those ideas. Such thoughts are part of a deadly scheme, the end of which is always death.

I can just hear some say, "She believes there exists an 'intelligence' behind evil? What is she, illiterate? This sounds like something out of *The Twilight Zone*."

In case you think I sound insane, stop and consider. One glance at the track record of moral evil in this world's hall of history horrors should convince you that it smells of something systematized. And systems don't just happen. They are devised. They are schemed. Behind them is intelligence.

Judaism, Christianity, Buddhism, Islam—they all recognize an intelligence behind moral evil.

Little wonder that Jesus not only recognized the existence of a devil, but nailed him with the name "tempter." Jesus called him that when the devil enticed Him to tell stones to become bread, to stand on the highest point of the temple and throw Himself down, and to bow down to the devil and worship him.[1]

And the tempter had one goal: murder. That's why, later on, Jesus nailed him again: "He was a murderer from the beginning, not holding to the truth, for there is no truth in him. When he lies, he speaks his native language, for he is a liar and the father of lies."[2]

The tempter. Murderer from the beginning. Father of lies. The devil's goal is to destroy your life, either by making your existence a living nightmare or by pushing you into an early grave. Take heed. If you have ever been enticed to prematurely end your life, then you've been listening not just to something but to someone. And just what are a few of the tempting lies he whispers?

"No One Cares"

One afternoon some time ago, I was sitting at my friend's coffee table, wrestling with whether I should tell her about the depression that had gripped me for several days. I decided to open up.

"Do you have time to listen?" I asked.

"Sure," she said, and promptly rose to retrieve a whistling teakettle from the stove. As she poured, I took a deep breath and started to unfold my problem.

Pause. "Milk in your tea?" Nod yes. Start again. Phone rings. "Wait a minute." Pick up where we left off. Knock at door. "What were you saying?" More distractions.

Friend half-listens. Friend gets up to warm tea.

Help. I hurt.

And this person couldn't care less.

Early on in his book *To Love Mercy*, Sam Storms wrote, "It's amazing how adept we . . . have become at getting along without each other."[3] And a little later, he wrote, "Beneath the water line of every life are the urges, motives, thoughts, fantasies, frustrated longings, crippling doubts, and sinful schemes of a fallen soul. This is where people are hurting. Tragically, though, we rarely encounter one another at such depth."[4]

It's true. Some people couldn't care less. Friends get preoccupied . . . nurses rush by your bed to tend to the next patient . . . neighbors never venture across the street to see how you're doing . . . families move apart and connect only occasionally over the phone.

In fact, you may feel no one cares for you. If so, those feelings might be justified. I've wheeled down nursing home hallways and peered into rooms, only to grieve to see lonely people sitting and staring, waiting for someone to visit them. Or you may be a lonely person who rubs shoulders with plenty of people all the time but has no intimate contact with any of them. Discussion about weather and sports may fill your day, while the real issues, the kind that eat at you when you lie awake thinking at night, stay harbored inside. You think, *Does anyone care?*

There *are* people who care. But it's possible you have built a self-imposed wall around you, a wall that allows absolutely no one inside to see what you're going through and to hurt with your hurts.

Your Creator never intended for you to shoulder a load of suffering by yourself. That's the whole purpose of spiritual community. God deliberately designed people to need each other. We must rub shoulders with people of hope and faith if our innermost needs are to be met.

And what if your relationships with those few friends aren't as open or as dependable as you'd like them to be? Then it may be up to you to do something about it. A community of people who give the kind of love that rolls up its sleeves can be created, if not found! A spontaneous, warm connection can develop with a chaplain in the hospital . . . a new friendship can happen with the kindly woman who visits your roommate . . . a fellowship can grow with those one or two people you always see praying in the hospital chapel . . . or maybe caring people can be found in that support group you've been avoiding.

That caring person may be a relative who is not so distant. An old friend you almost forgot about. A coworker who used to invite you to lunch now and then. People who care can be found in homeless shelters. Meetings of Alcoholics Anonymous. Parents Without Partners. Weight Watchers. Disability associations. Churches.

Someone cares.

"There's Nothing More to Expect from Life"

This is another standard lie, and it's a tempting thought, especially when you can't see beyond the thick, gray fog of hopelessness that has settled around you. But it's still a lie. There *is* life on the other side of that fog.

Viktor Frankl put it this way:

> In the concentration camp, I remember two cases of
> would-be suicide which bore a striking similarity. Both used
> the typical argument—they had nothing more to expect from
> life. In both cases it was a question of getting them to realize
> that *life was still expecting something from them* . . .
>
> We found in fact that for the one, it was his child whom
> he adored . . . for the other it was a thing, not a person. This
> man was a scientist and had written a series of books which
> still needed to be finished . . . A man who becomes conscious
> of the responsibility he bears toward a human being who
> affectionately waits for him, or to an unfinished work, will
> never be able to throw away his life. He knows the "why"
> for his existence, and will be able to bear almost any "how."[5]

You may not be expecting anything from life, but life is still
anticipating something from you. As with the man in the concentration camp, your responsibility may be to a child, perhaps a
grandchild or the young boy next door. Your decision to die or not
to die has a powerful impact on the mind of a child.

In the movie *The Boy Who Could Fly*, a father who felt he
had nothing to give in the face of a cancer diagnosis ended his
life prematurely, leaving behind two children, Milly and Louis.
Louis became withdrawn and sullen. Leaning on his elbows, the
teary-eyed boy mumbled about his father's demise, "He didn't even
try, Milly. Why didn't he try?" The father's decision had a lasting
and negative impact on that child's life. Fictional, yes, but the boy's
response is easy to believe.

In a real-life example, a friend of mine named Carol Swegle had
everything: a rich husband, a beauty queen title, a gorgeous country

home, wealthy friends, and loving children. But Carol became depressed and tried to find relief in a combination of prescription drugs and alcohol. She had pinned all of her hopes on a little bit of fame and a small fortune, only to discover emptiness. One day in her bedroom, she held a gun and readied herself to pull the trigger. At that instant, her children burst into the room and startled her. The gun went off.

Carol fell to the floor, a quadriplegic. She lost her husband, her house, and her friends, and she ended up living in a nursing home. If ever there were a time to pull a trigger, it would have been then! But Carol hung on to the hope of claiming back her children. Her daughters gave her reason enough to try again.

In the end? Although it was true that her children were seriously affected by her suicide attempt, in the long run, through Carol's perseverance and changed attitude, her decision to live became her children's redemption. They were reunited.

Life, perhaps in the person of a child, is still expecting something from you.

Or then again, perhaps as it comes to expression in the form of a particular thing, life is anticipating more from you. I receive letters from prisoners, disabled people in institutions, and elderly folks who often send poems, small paintings, crayoned drawings, crocheted bookmarks, pot holders . . . whatever. These things are creative expressions of one person to another person—to me. Scribbled drawings and tattered bookmarks are expressions of the soul, and these simple things tie this person to the rest of the world.

"I Can't Live with This Depression"

You don't have to believe this lie. Admittedly, nothing distorts reality like depression. A blowup with your husband has you discounting twenty years of a good marriage. A little headache has you wondering if you've got brain cancer. A diagnosis of a serious illness has you digging your grave the next day. It's amazing how quickly reality gets turned upside down when you're depressed.

But I was impressed with the way this teen approached her depression:

> Dear Joni,
>
> My name is Katherine, and I'll be fourteen in four days. It also marks my first year in my wheelchair. I've lost the use of my legs and one arm forever. (The arm part is my own fault though.) I wouldn't do my therapy because I was so depressed over my bleak future.
>
> Now I've discovered I need God's love more than ever. I want to start off talking with someone who knows what I'm going through. Please help me find the love a Christian knows.
>
> > Love,
> > Katherine

Katherine is barely in her teens, has lived in a wheelchair for a year, and yet devotes not more than one line to her depression. Most of us would devote an entire page!

When I wrote Katherine back, I shared how even stained-glass window saints like the apostles got depressed. The apostle Paul wrote to his friends, "We are pressed on every side by troubles, but not crushed and broken. We are perplexed because we don't know why things happen as they do, but we don't give up and quit. We are hunted down, but God never abandons us. We get knocked down, but we get up again and keep going."[6]

There's a little bit of that attitude in Katherine. Somehow

after hitting rock bottom, she was able to get up again and keep going. I'm sure it took time to work through her sorrow, grief, and limitations, but somewhere in the fog of hopelessness, she found a thin ray of hope.

It's called faith. You don't need much more than the mustard-seed-sized faith of a fourteen-year-old girl. True, Katherine, like most of us, will face even tougher times in the future, but she has begun to learn to choose her attitude and to invest her life in others. In so doing, she will be able to live courageously, no matter what her feelings.

"Nothing Awaits Me after Death"

This could be the biggest lie of all.

And this is exactly why the devil enjoys helping you scheme your own murder. Does that sound harsh? You may call it self-deliverance or aid-in-dying if you wish. It matters little to the devil; it's all murder to him.

Moreover, it matters little whether or not you believe in hell. The devil doesn't care whether you label it "a white light at the end of a tunnel" or "nirvana" or "never-never land." It's all hell to him.

And what is it like? Fire and brimstone? A black hole? A bleak nothingness? The devil once again shrugs his shoulders at such descriptions. All that matters to him is that hell is separation—total and final—from God. Hell is misery, deeper and more profound than any misery you could experience on earth. And because misery loves company, the devil wants to take as many with him to hell as he possibly can. That includes you.

Frankly, it's enough that Jesus believed in hell, and He spoke of it more often than He did of heaven. Without my going into a lot of detail here, Jesus simply warned, "It is better for you to enter life maimed or crippled than to have two hands or two feet and be thrown into eternal fire."[7]

The tempter would have you believe it's not that bad a place. And just how does the devil beguile you into hell before you can find heaven? His strategy reminds me of a letter I read that described advice given to a man dying from AIDS:

> Dear Editor,
>
> A terminally ill AIDS patient recently called the Hemlock Society of North Texas. He was suffering greatly . . . In our phone conversations, his anguish over the conviction that he would probably go to hell also came out.
>
> I told him of my own and other beliefs, which differ greatly, on this subject. I described a recent survey which shows that about 50 percent of all Americans believe in the existence of hell, but only about 4 percent think they are likely to go there. With the help from my friendly local librarian, I obtained a copy of this survey to send him, along with the Drug Dosage Table of the National Hemlock Society.
>
> This may be the first time the Society has helped someone to carry out a "double self-deliverance," both from a harsh terminal illness and from a harsh theological conviction.
>
> The Hemlock Society
> of North Texas[8]

This person with AIDS was told the truth about how to kill himself with lethal drugs, but he wasn't told the truth about hell. The letter was an eerie cover-up of the facts. Do you believe that nothing awaits you after death? Would you be willing to stake your life on it? Of all the questions to be settled before you take the final exit, this issue is paramount. So take a long, hard look at the consequences of a decision that is so fatal and, worst of all, so final.

If you think hell is fiction, then say so. But if you have even an inkling that it may be real, then wake up. Leave no stone unturned, no means untried, until you find life worth living both on this side of eternity and on the other.

Don't Believe Lies

The devil will go to great lengths to charm you into an early grave. Everything from pushing drug dosage tables in your face to pooh-poohing hell as pure nonsense. He'll move all of hell (and heaven if he could) to stop your heartbeat and have you pronounced dead.

Let's unmask his way of operating.

This morning I was having a rough start to my day. My chronic pain made it impossible to get comfortable in my wheelchair. I shook my head and growled, "This body is a pain. I hate it!"

Why was that so awful? Because the enemy has a deep hatred of my body, and all I was doing was agreeing with him. He gets a charge out of my verbal barbs about my body. And he would like to get you to do the same. Whether you are approaching the final throes of a terminal illness or you're deep in depression, the devil delights in hearing us bad-mouth our bodies.

Why? Because your body, even underneath wrinkles or fat, and in spite of the ravages of illness or old age, is made in the image of God. Your heart, mind, hands, and feet are stamped with the imprint of the Creator. Little wonder the devil wants you to do your body in!

This morning I had to once again plug my ears against the lies of the tempter and remember that I am, as David writes in Psalm

139:14, "fearfully and wonderfully made." I rehearsed the old, familiar truth that God has a plan for this flesh and blood of mine. That's why the devil considers my body a threat. He understands that when I yield my body to God, though it may be paralyzed, my feet and hands are powerful weapons against his forces of darkness.

Listen to the Truth

By the way, the devil would have you believe a couple more lies. He wants to convince you that he is either a powerless "elf gone bad" in a red suit with a funny tail or an evenly matched and almost-as-mighty opponent of God.

Neither is true.

The devil is only a fallen angel.[9]

He is a deceiver.[10]

He is doomed for destruction.[11]

And until then, he has one goal in mind: your destruction.

Questions for Discussion and Reflection
Liar, Liar . . .

Just this once, you get to practice lying. Consider the following situations, and develop a lie that Satan would tell each person.

Satan's lie to . . .

- a teenage girl with cerebral palsy (a disability that can restrict motion and speech and affect physical appearance)
- a forty-year-old man with Down syndrome (a form of intellectual disability—what many used to call "mental retardation")
- an eighty-year-old man in a nursing home
- the parents of a four-year-old son in a coma
- a disabled child of a parent just filing for divorce

1. What is Satan's purpose in telling such lies?
2. Why does Satan want society to be deceived? What is the evidence that such deception has occurred?
3. What does the Bible say about defending ourselves and others against such lies?

Chapter 7

YOUR DECISION
MATTERS TO GOD

To this you were called, because Christ suffered for you,
leaving you an example, that you should follow in his steps.
1 PETER 2:21

Whenever I begin to think my efforts don't count—or even when my quadriplegia and wheelchair feel like too much to handle—I think of a young woman named Kim.

I first learned about Kim when an elder from her church in Pennsylvania called to ask if I would contact her with a few words of encouragement. "Kim is a brilliant twenty-six-year-old Christian woman who has always been active in our church," he said, "but last year she contracted a motor-neuron disease and now must stay in bed. She can hardly move and must be fed with a feeding tube." The elder paused for a moment and then added, "Kim is very depressed, and she's wondering if her life is worth living anymore."

I telephoned Kim right away. Her mother tucked the receiver

under her ear. Her breathing was so faint that I could hardly hear Kim's voice. We discussed many things, including our favorite parts of the Bible, the subject of heaven, and prayer. Finally, Kim said with great labor, "Joni, they want to give me a ventilator to help me breathe, but I don't know whether I want one. I'm so tired. Do you think I should go on a ventilator?"

I was speechless. I took a deep breath, whispered a prayer, and replied, "Kim, there are a lot of things to consider, not the least of which is that your decision will affect many people around you. But of the two choices facing you, I think there's a better one." I then proceeded to share with her a simple but powerful Bible verse that has encouraged and guided me through the *toughest* of times in my fifty years of quadriplegia.

Second Peter 3:8 reads, "Do not forget this one thing, dear friends: With the Lord a day is like a thousand years, and a thousand years are like a day." We all know the old adage that God looks at the last two thousand years as a couple of days gone by, I told her, but what about the other half of the verse? The part about seeing each day as a thousand years? It's like divine arithmetic. It doesn't take a rocket scientist to figure out God's mathematical formula. If we see each day as comparable to a millennium in eternity, then *each twenty-four hours is chock full of opportunities to invest in a thousand years' worth of eternity*. Each day God gives us the precious gift of hours to invest in the lives of others—investments that will have eternal repercussions for us and them.

Kim perked up at this idea. "But I'm in bed. I can't go anywhere or do anything. How can my life count in this condition?" This is what I told her: "First, Kim, you can pray. No matter how feeble or fainthearted your prayers may seem, they have very special power with God. Psalm 10:17 reads, 'You, LORD, hear the desire of the afflicted; you encourage them, and you listen to their cry.' The Lord cups his ear to listen when someone like you prays, someone who is enduring great affliction. He bends over backward when people offer him a sacrifice of praise. God is going to use your intercessions to shake the lives of everyone around you."

That intrigued her. "And your obedience counts for eternity. Now is your chance to stretch your soul's capacity for God, Kim. Your patience and endurance will resound to more glory to God than you can possibly appreciate right now. As the apostle Paul writes in Romans 8:18, 'I consider that our present sufferings are not worth comparing with the glory that will be revealed in us.' If you keep a godly response, then it must multiply out to at least 558 years of eternal benefit to you and glory to God!"

She laughed, and I shared more. I encouraged her to think of the impact her patience and endurance would have on others around her, like her mom and dad. Philippians 2:4 tells us to always look out for the interests of others before our own. We are *always* called to think of others, no matter how difficult our circumstances.

I suggested to Kim, "The next time your mother tube-feeds you your lunch, why don't you ask to say a blessing on the food before she syringes it into your G-tube? Do the divine math on that one. It's got to pan out to at least 784 years' worth of eternal benefit to you and your mother, as well as glory to God."

What a way for Kim to live out her remaining days! She became a living example of 2 Corinthians 4:16–18: "Therefore we do not lose heart. Though outwardly we are wasting away, yet inwardly we are being renewed day by day. For our light and momentary troubles are achieving for us an eternal glory that far outweighs them all. So we fix our eyes not on what is seen, but on what is unseen, since what is seen is temporary, but what is unseen is eternal."

Kim ended up living another month and a half after our conversation on the phone. But as her mother told me later, those forty-five days—she looked at them as forty-five thousand years—were some of the most meaningful and important weeks she ever lived.

Friend, if Kim made the most of every opportunity to reflect Jesus Christ during those difficult last days of her life, you and I can reflect Jesus as well.

Perhaps you're not facing the decision to accept a ventilator or refuse it. You may not be dying, debilitated, or terminally ill. But still, you'd give anything to feel the peace Kim found. Trouble is, you still might be tempted to believe the lie that peace is found by prematurely ending your life.

True, you may feel that no one seems to care. And maybe not a soul does care! You may feel as though life is not expecting a single thing from you, and you simply cannot live with depression. Sadly, you are even willing to stake your life on the belief that nothing awaits you after death.

If so, you *need* peace! But remember, peace of mind comes not in the form of a death sentence, but through people. There is a Person who cares about you, even if no one else does. He calls Himself the Prince of Peace. And it is His perspective on life I want to talk to you about.

The Bible Speaks Out on Euthanasia

You may think that euthanasia of people who are dying or disabled is a rather recent phenomenon, but not so. The Old Testament records an incident involving King Saul of Israel, who became seriously wounded on the battlefield. Fearing the advancing enemy, Saul took his own sword and tried to fall on it. He cried out to a soldier, "Come and put me out of my misery . . . for I am in terrible pain but life lingers on." The soldier deferred to the wishes of the king and killed him. Then, acting most likely on his supposed innocence, he brought some of Saul's armor to David and said, "So I killed him, for I knew he couldn't live."[1]

There were no laws on the books back then about assisted suicide, but that did not stop David from banging the gavel of Israel's justice. He ordered the soldier put to death. Perhaps onlookers were shocked by the verdict. After all, Saul was dying anyway. He was in great pain, and if captured, he feared torture and abuse in his final hours. These things were probably on the mind of the soldier who performed the mercy killing, but his actions stand in contrast with the response of Saul's bodyguard, who, minutes earlier, had been too terrified to commit the act.[2]

To be fair, it seems that Saul's status as king of Israel added to the guilt of the deed, and David was outraged that someone had the nerve to harm the king who was anointed by God. But I believe it's fair to draw a principle that is as true for people today as it was for people several thousand years ago. Whether for a monarch or a common man, carrying out a mercy killing is wrong; the fact that Saul was king only heightened the criminality of the soldier's deed.[3]

God clearly opposes *active euthanasia*, whether it involves plunging a sword into the bleeding body of a king on a battlefield or plunging a syringe full of phenobarbital into the veins of a dying patient. The prohibition against murder in the Ten Commandments logically includes murder of the self.[4] Mercy killing, whether committed actively or passively, is always presented in a negative light in the Bible. In Scripture, people who either killed themselves or sought to be put out of their misery are always seen as disobedient.[5]

And as for those who will say, "I'll do with my body as I wish," God has a response: "You are not your own; you were bought at a price. Therefore honor God with your bodies."[6]

No, there's no biblical account of someone refusing medical treatment to cause death. But what we do have is the example of Jesus and the choices He made in His dying. When Jesus was hanging on His cross, He was offered one drink—which He refused—and a second, which He accepted. Did He change His mind? No, the first drink offered Him was wine mixed with myrrh, a narcotic drink.[7] The second was a sour wine vinegar, a drink intended to relieve thirst more effectively than plain water.[8] David Mathis writes, "This first wine represented an offer to ease the pain, to opt for a small shortcut . . . But this offer Jesus refused . . . And the second (sour) wine was given to keep him 'conscious for as long as possible,' and thus have the effect of prolonging his pain. This is the wine Jesus drank."[9]

Similarly, Dr. John MacArthur says of the second offered drink, "On the one hand this would quench a momentary thirst but over the long haul it could . . . [bring] the kind of refreshment that allowed a person to live a little bit longer."[10]

So very much was accomplished in the death of Jesus, and I'm not saying that in His death, Jesus made a definitive statement on end-of-life choices. Yes, Jesus was an example for us, as 1 Peter 2:21 tells us, but His example encompasses far more than our end-of-life choices. What I *am* saying is that Jesus did not allow the threat of prolonged suffering to influence His decisions. Jesus chose not to sidestep suffering—not to take a shortcut—but instead to meet pain head-on.

In short? The Bible teaches that any means to produce or hasten death in order to alleviate suffering is never justified. Or in the language of the Bible, it is never right to do evil.[11]

The Bible Speaks Out on Dying

However, *letting someone die* is another matter entirely. Allowing a person to die when he or she is, in fact, dying is justified. The Bible is full of examples of people doing all they can to help a person live, but when it came time for a person to die, Scripture doesn't do much more than record the death. No paramedics were called to the scene, no CPR administered, no Heimlich maneuver carried out. The Old and New Testaments do not specifically address many of our present-day problems and questions related to "letting someone die." Scripture is probably silent because those problems didn't exist in biblical times. There were no ventilators, drug therapies, pacemakers, or feeding tubes to confuse the difference between prolonging the process of dying and sustaining life.

In fact, the Bible speaks about death not in technical terms, but in the everyday language of ordinary experience. Today, doctors generally agree that a person is dead if the functions of the brain and brain stem cease, but Scripture does not formally define death in those terms or any others. It simply assumes we understand what death is.

But what Scripture lacks in absolute definitions, it makes up for in absolute decrees. There's a kind of medical dictionary exactness to a verse like Job 14:5: "A person's days are determined; you have decreed the number of his months and have set limits he cannot exceed."

That verse, along with others, rightly influences our judgments. "Keeping a comatose person alive by a machine, one who has an incurable disease and is irreversibly dying, is unnecessary," writes evangelical theologian Norman Geisler in his book *Christian Ethics.* "In fact, it could be viewed as unethical . . . Extraordinary efforts to fight the divinely appointed limits of our mortality are really working in opposition to God."[12]

Exchange Fear for Peace

People's intense interest in euthanasia can be summed up in one word: fear. Ever since the days of Eden, we've been haunted by fear of each side of the grave we look at. As the old song goes, "I'm tired of living and scared of dying."[13] On this side of the tombstone, our fears are aggravated by strange new diseases, machines that dehumanize, and treatments that rob dignity. Yet peering beyond the tombstone, we're afraid of the abyss—the unknowable hereafter.

Peace is the opposite of fear. As I shared earlier, we are all in search of peace when it comes to life and death decisions. And the Prince of Peace is the only one who can rid us of fear, no matter which side of the grave we look at. The Bible calms our fears with these words:

> Since we, God's children, are human beings—made of flesh and blood—he became flesh and blood too by being born in human form; for only as a human being could he die and in dying break the power of the devil who had the power of death. Only in that way could he deliver those who through fear of death have been living all their lives as slaves to constant dread.[14]

Read it again. God became a human being—that's Jesus. Jesus, through His death, broke the power of the devil and his lies. He also wants to deliver you from your fears, whether fear of life as a living nightmare or fear of death as a permanent and total separation from God. To believe in Jesus gives you peace in the here and now and peace about the hereafter.

How? Well, remember that scary abyss? What makes it so foreboding is our guilt. And guilt is no psychological fiction: you've broken Somebody's law and no matter how much others may flatter you on the outside, on the inside a guilty conscience nails you for lust, pride, and prejudice, just to name a few. The punishment for breaking the law is death. But like the verse says, Jesus *delivers*!

When He bore God's punishment, Jesus raised His cross as a sign marker, arranging a right turn away from hell and into heaven.

To place your hand in the hand of the Prince of Peace does not necessarily guarantee protection from suffering, nor does it offer immunity from difficult deathbed decisions. But it does give you a steadfast hand to hold on to, including the certainty that a loving and all-powerful God who knows everything is standing by your side. Putting your confidence in Christ will free you from living your whole life as a slave to constant dread—dread of facing life as a living nightmare, and dread of facing death as the dark unknown.

God loves life. He despises death, for "the last enemy to be destroyed is death."[15] Jesus said, "My purpose is to give life in all its fullness"—life not only in the here and now, but in the hereafter.[16] There are good reasons why God wants you to live. He wants you to have peace. He knows your life can have value in the here and now. And He wants you to choose the joys of heaven.

God Knows You're Heading for a Hereafter

If you were to ask the brother and sister duo Paige and Tyson Snedeker which truth from the Bible gave them the most peace in the midst of their ever-increasing limitations, they may very well respond with Romans 8:18: "I consider that our present sufferings are not worth comparing with the glory that will be revealed in us."

That's saying a mouthful! Some people find it difficult to think realistically about heaven. Even the spiritually minded feel awkward working toward "eternity" because it seems so far away, almost unreal. Even when we try to imagine what it would be like, we come up short of having a real desire to go there. Who wants to live forever tucked behind a galaxy where birds chirp, organs resound, and angels bounce from cloud to cloud?

If that were a true picture of heaven, an awful lot of people would be lukewarm about going there.

The fact is, descriptions of heaven aren't as important as grasping the *fact* of heaven. Heaven is the place where God is going to give His family the biggest welcome-home party in history. Entrance into heaven means no more suffering, no more tears, and a life free from pain and filled with joy. Perhaps that's why people who are dying, debilitated, or terminally ill are often those most ready to believe in God. Maybe the devil couldn't care less about whether or not you believe in hell, but God definitely cares whether or not you believe in heaven!

Believing in Jesus is the first step to a life that goes far beyond this world. Once that fundamental point is settled, there are a few facts we can hold on to until we cross the other side of the grave and step into a bright eternity with God.

You were made for one purpose: to make God real to those around you. Don't think He has left you without any means whatsoever for fulfilling that end just because you are confined to bed or struggling with pain. In a mysterious way, each day you live; each hopeful thought you think, however fleeting; each smile you muster—all of it brings God incredible joy. That's because your positive attitude and actions, however small and faint, are fingers pointing others to a God who is larger and finer and grander than they thought. That's what it means to glorify Him as you lie in that bed, sit in that wheelchair, or persevere through that depression.

Your suffering has meaning now and forever. This is what Romans 8:18 is all about. Your present suffering isn't worth comparing with the glory that will be revealed in you. How can that be? Loneliness, feelings of total abandonment, pain, and the like are capable of being exchanged for something precious, eternal, weighty, and real—so much so that it's hardly worth comparing the two. God will one day reward you for enduring suffering with an uncomplaining attitude. When you exchange anger for faith in Him, then your life in heaven will be larger, finer, and grander because of that very suffering.

God works in your life up until the final moment. It may appear that nothing is taking place in the life of a dying loved one, an individual in a coma, or someone with a severe disability, but God is not hindered from accomplishing His work in a life just because nothing seems to be happening. The work of God is spiritual activity, often separated a long way from one's cerebral, neurological, or muscular activity. Only eternity will reveal the work that was accomplished.

Life is more fleeting than we realize. We act as though this world is all there is. It's little wonder we don't care about eternity. We need the perspective of David, who wrote these words in Psalm 39:4–6:

> Show me, LORD, my life's end
>> and the number of my days;
>> let me know how fleeting my life is.
> You have made my days a mere handbreadth;
>> the span of my years is as nothing before you . . .
> Surely everyone goes around like a mere phantom;
>> in vain they rush about, heaping up wealth
>> without knowing whose it will finally be.

The brevity of life ought to open our eyes to what it means to live beyond time. When you put your pain in that perspective, not only does time seem shortened, but suffering has an end in sight.

Dying is your final passage. The stripping away of all human powers, mental as well as physical, is a part of the process that George MacDonald calls "undressing for its last sweet bed."[17]

When we who believe in God die, we leave behind our claim on our earthly "clothes" and become clothed with immortality.[18]

God knows we're heading for a hereafter. For those who, apart from Him, prematurely end their lives, hoping to find relief, there will only be a hereafter of vast and utter disappointment. For those who believe in Jesus, the dying process becomes the most significant passage of their lives. Theirs is a hereafter of more joy than they could possibly imagine.

God Knows You Have Value in the Here and Now

I once cornered Dr. J. I. Packer, a prominent evangelical theologian, and asked him this question: "What would you say about a man whose cerebral palsy has left him totally bedridden, nonverbal, and relegated to a back bedroom in a nursing home? No one visits him, and no nurse takes time to benefit from his good attitude. What can that man do?" I knew plenty of real-life examples, so the question wasn't hypothetical.

Dr. Packer folded his hands, thought for a moment, and then replied, "A man like that can worship and glorify God."

That response almost sounded as though Dr. Packer was piously patting this man on the head and trivializing his plight with a platitude that was too heavenly minded. But I've encountered enough people who are isolated and limited, like the man with cerebral palsy I used as an example, to know that Dr. Packer is right, and I've looked into the Bible long enough to know his advice is well taken.

I think of Tracy Traylor, a beautiful blonde-haired college student who suffered a severe head injury and was in a coma for five and a half months. She came out of it unable to walk or talk well enough for people outside her family to understand her.

I met Tracy and her mother at a conference. Tracy, sitting slumped in her wheelchair, slightly lifted her bobbing head and shoved something in her lap toward me. It was a necklace made of clay and colored beads, and one of the clay pieces had an imprint of a leaping deer.

"Oh, Tracy," I said, "this is beautiful. Thank you for the gift."

"My daughter was a design student in college, and she directs me on how to craft each piece of jewelry," her mother proudly explained. I could hardly imagine the enormous effort it took for the two of them to communicate.

Just then, I noticed some words typed on a piece of paper twist-tied to the necklace. They were from Isaiah 35:4, 6: "Your God will come . . . Then will the lame leap like a deer." I couldn't hold back the tears. Tracy and I have enjoyed a marvelous friendship since that day. We both delight in taking the leaping-deer necklaces she makes and sharing them with other folks who eagerly await God's coming. Although Tracy can hardly speak, her smile and her witness speak volumes. Her brilliant and shining hope has cast long, lingering shadows on me.

I know that hundreds of people rush by Tracy in her wheelchair, each of them oblivious to the powerful message she carries with her. Maybe millions of people wouldn't care one iota about this woman's lovely attitude, but Someone far more significant cares, and He has a purpose: "The purpose is that all the angelic powers should now see the complex wisdom of God's plan being worked out through the Church."[19]

Whether a godly attitude shines from a young woman with a brain injury or from a lonely man relegated to a back bedroom, the response of patience and perseverance counts. God points to the peaceful attitude of suffering people to teach others about Himself. Not only is He teaching those we rub shoulders with every day, but He is also instructing the countless millions of angels and demons. The hosts in heaven stand amazed when they watch God sustain hurting people with His peace.

It matters to God not only *that* you live, but *how* you live.

God Can Be Trusted Even When There Are No Reasons

The message was scribbled and rain splattered: "Laurel Ledford needs to talk to you." We met in an office at the retreat center where I was speaking. I was surprised when she entered the room carrying her three-month-old baby. It was cold and windy, not the kind of day to run errands with an infant. But then again, it wasn't easy for Laurel to find someone to babysit her son with spina bifida. She sat across from me in a heavy sweater, holding her child bundled in blankets.

Laurel relayed her story—one incident after another of heart-twisting disappointment. First they moved after selling all they had so her husband, Steve, could go to school. Then their baby boy, Stephen, was born. Next she carried and lost a baby girl. Then again. Immediately after the loss of this second child, she accidentally became pregnant. When she was six months along, her husband had surgery, which further drained their already limited bank account.

She tugged at her little boy's blanket and in tears said, "I thought I could handle losing another baby, but I could definitely not handle a baby with a birth defect. Shortly after that, my doctor told me that the baby I was carrying had severe hydrocephalus and spina bifida. He told me that one option would be to have a spontaneous delivery."

"You mean abortion?"

Laurel nodded. I mentally added the phrase "spontaneous delivery" to that list of pleasant-sounding euphemisms.

"But I would *not* choose to lose my baby," she said. "Still, that's when depression and thoughts of suicide came to mind. I spent a long, gray Midwestern winter on the couch watching a lot of TV."

Laurel went on to say that after the birth of David, her baby with spina bifida, she struggled with more feelings of hopelessness. "David's head size looked terrible, and I was struggling with bonding. I didn't want him or even like him. I had so much guilt and confusion—"

I had to interrupt. "What kept you going?"

Laurel hiked David up on her lap to think. "I plastered our walls with Scriptures. Psalm 34 says, 'The LORD is close to the brokenhearted and saves those who are crushed in spirit.'" Then she paused for another long moment. "But sometimes I still get so depressed. There's no rhyme or reason for why all these awful things have happened."

She had a point. Any information I might have given Laurel at that moment would have come off sounding like clichés. Sometimes the magnitude of a person's suffering seems to outweigh any potential benefit. The puzzle of suffering doesn't always get completed. There are sometimes no reasons that will satisfy. As Laurel pressed her lips to the bulging forehead of little David, I thought of Deuteronomy 29:29: "The secret things belong to the LORD our God."

"Joni," Laurel said, startling me from my thoughts, "how do I face tomorrow?" Her liquid brown eyes looked at me with such pleading.

I took a deep breath. "I have to confess I wonder the same thing. I get weak-kneed thinking about the future stretching on and on in front of me. But God does not expect me to accept what may or may not happen to me years from now."

Laurel gave a questioning look.

"God doesn't give strength to face next year's headaches or even next month's heartaches. He won't even loan you enough strength to face tomorrow. He only gives you and me strength to face today. To live one day at a time."

She nodded in understanding.

"I'm sure that's why Jesus said, 'Do not worry about tomorrow, for tomorrow will worry about itself. Each day has enough trouble of its own.'[20] You'll have to face tomorrow, Laurel, without answers to your questions. The best you and I can do is hold on to the One who holds the answers."

We spent the rest of our time together in silence, mostly listening to David breathe softly and sigh every once in a while. We both sensed that enough words had been spoken. Yet in the quiet, a bond was growing between us. After a while, we hugged and said good-bye.

A month or so later, I received a letter from Laurel. Life had not gotten easier. One evening, her son Stephen disappeared. She was sick with panic. Neighbors were telephoned and the police contacted. A search began. When Laurel heard a patrol car calling for the K-9 unit, she fell apart. She said, "It was as if a demon was screaming into my ears, 'Do it now! Kill yourself! End it now!'"

A half hour later, her son was found. He had been hiding in the house the whole time.

Why? What reason could there possibly be for the torment and pain? There's no answer. But I noticed a P.S. at the close of her letter, a message that was better than any answer: "I'm trying to reach out to at least one person a day and do something for them that counts for eternity. It works!"

Your Decision Matters to a Personal God

Laurel heard the devil screeching in her ear one moment, and God whispering in her other ear the next. Should she shut her ears to the devil's lies, or should she wall herself off from God's words? Laurel teeters almost daily on the edge of eternity—that's why she sees every day as a choice. And her decision goes far beyond whether she should "Do it now! End your life!"

Laurel and many like her who have been tempted to sidestep all the suffering grit their teeth and decide daily to live. For these friends, life has value both now and in the hereafter.

It's something they remind themselves of each day. It's a decision they act on, a decision that matters to God.

Questions for Discussion and Reflection
In Heaven's Eyes

In the discussion and reflection section of the last chapter, you spent time lying. Now you get to be a reporter for heaven! On the left are hypothetical headlines from planet Earth. Opposite each headline from *Earth's Gazette*, write a contrasting headline of victory from heaven's perspective for *Heaven's Hope*, the angels' daily newspaper. The first headline has been provided as an example.

Earth's Gazette	*Heaven's Hope*
Supreme Court upholds assisted suicide as constitutional	Assisted suicide declared a passing fad as thousands of Christians provide friendships and assistance to persons with disabilities
First 24-hour euthanasia clinic opens in Toledo	
Abortion named as the number one reason for dramatic decline in children born with disabilities	
Thousands of disabled denied health care by the Health Rationing Committee	

Consider the following scenario:

Barbara is a young Christian in the last stages of Lou Gehrig's disease. She is totally paralyzed, and for her, the next step will be a ventilator to help her breathe. She wants to do what God wants but is unsure whether or not to get "hooked up."

1. What would you tell her?

2. Have you ever had to trust God when there seemed to be no reason for the crisis you were facing? What was it that brought you through?

Part Three

A TIME
TO DIE

Chapter 8

SUSTAINING LIFE, BUT NOT PROLONGING DEATH

If I expect life to be unending, then dying seems to be an illusion. If I live life as a vocation, then dying is an intrusion. If life is a threat, then dying is an escape. If I accept life as a gift, then dying is a part of the given.
GLEN DAVIDSON

My father should have been raised as a cowboy on the open plains. Actually, he almost was. Born in 1900, he led a rough-rider life, trading with Native Americans in the Northwest and scaling the highest peaks of the Rockies. I loved following in his footsteps, riding fast horses, hiking high mountains, and camping under the moon and stars. Dad was my hero.

When I was little, he took me and my sisters to see a movie about Eskimos called *The Savage Innocents.* I was troubled by a scene in which an elderly Eskimo who was dying was left behind on an ice floe. We talked about it on the way home, and although I can't remember my father's words, I knew Daddy probably would have chosen the same path.

I forgot about that movie until decades later when my father became physically and mentally debilitated by a series of strokes that left him virtually bedridden. It was the long-feared nightmare that we, while growing up, always pushed from our minds. Our ninety-year-old dad was but a shadow of his former self. His withered, bony frame couldn't hide the undaunted spirit that twinkled from his blue eyes, and it crushed our hearts to think that Daddy was probably going to die within a year—maybe months or even weeks.

The family house in Maryland was sold. Mother moved Dad and herself to Florida, where he resided in a cheery little nursing home. Mom walked from my uncle's house to the nursing home every morning to care for her husband's needs and then returned at night after he was in bed. My sisters and I often visited, and Linda, Jay, and Kathy frequently stretched their visits so they could help our mother and dad.

Then, in a span of less than two weeks, everything changed. My father began to quickly fail. He was rushed to the hospital. An IV was inserted. The tube was later removed when his body bloated and his lungs filled. He was sent back to the nursing home. Our family collapsed in exhaustion. We agonized and conferred with doctors. After much prayer and painful discussion, we made a decision: no feeding tube. It was clear Daddy was dying, and knowing my father, he would not want the process of his dying prolonged. My sisters and mom tenderly cared for Daddy around the clock during his last days, camping on couch pillows by his bedside and giving him what little water he could take in.

In that little nursing home, my mother had sat vigil with Dad for more than a year and a half, helping him daily and spreading the joy of the Lord to every elderly person up and down each hallway. In his last week, I joined my sisters and Mom there. It was obvious Dad was failing fast.

I had to leave after a few days. It was a tearful departure, knowing I'd never see my father again on this side of eternity.

Within days, I received a phone call from Jay.

Daddy had passed away.

My sister told me how Dad had turned to my mother, opened both his blue eyes for the first time in days, gave her a big smile, and languished for a moment in what they emphatically described as a "glow." It must have been the glow of God's presence, because then . . . he took his last breath and passed away.

My mother, sisters, a recreational therapist, and a nurse held hands around his bed and sang a doxology. I knew it was a fitting end to Daddy's life. From there, my sisters canvassed the hallways, telling people, "Daddy just went to heaven to be with the Lord. Isn't that exciting?"

When It Comes to Dying, We Need the Wisdom of God

Who would have dreamed the day would come when the family of a dying loved one would have to study a medical dictionary to discern exactly what "dying" was. We all wish dying were as simple as "Naked I came from my mother's womb, and naked I will depart. The LORD gave and the LORD has taken away."[1]

It seems like it *should* be simple. God gives life; God takes life away—and there's a line between the two. But where is the line? Has modern technology thrown a monkey wrench into the way

God gives and takes life? Has modern medicine presented God with problems to which even He has no answer?

If God has given man tools with which to sustain life, it would seem impossible to outrun His wisdom. God, by nature, can't say, "Well, people, I don't know what to do about those machines and treatments you've invented. They're new to Me. You'll have to make those decisions in your realm because I can't comprehend it all, much less offer wisdom."

God doesn't operate that way. If He provides man with the talent to advance and invent on behalf of life, He must also provide the wisdom to make decisions. And the question begging wisdom is this: *What is the distinction between providing a person with all the life to which they're entitled as opposed to artificially prolonging the process of their death?*

Most of us wish that someone else would do the moral choosing for us, just explaining flat-out the differences. Some people look for wisdom by polling the majority, asking what "most people" would do. Others go with their gut feelings, ranging in degree of certainty from "I think I know what's best, but don't ask me to explain it" to "I'm absolutely right about this." Many people rely on their conscience, which is a little better than going by feelings, but it still falls short. None of these are reliable because feelings vary, the majority is often wrong, and an armor of conscience is only as dependable as its weakest piece. There must be a better place to find wisdom.

God Gives Necessary Wisdom for a Particular Problem

The Bible is full of God's wisdom. And from it we can derive wisdom—defined in the dictionary as the "power of judging rightly and following the soundest course of action based on knowledge, experience, understanding, etc."

First, there are definite dos and don'ts in Scripture. "You shall not murder" is pretty straightforward. However, when there are no scriptural commands, you're forced to look closer. Some actions are commendable; some are permitted; and some are prohibited by Scripture. The Bible is a big book, and it takes a little research to decipher between the "don't dos" and the "maybe dos."

Second, since the Bible is a book to be applied in practical living, we next need to consider the many different situations that a person can face today. Use of a ventilator may be good in one situation and bad in another. Kidney dialysis may be appropriate for one person but not the next. Chemotherapy may be great for some but wrong for others. Lower limb amputation may be considered an ordinary procedure on a forty-seven-year-old with diabetes, but on a ninety-year-old, it may be a futile and burdensome one.

Once we have considered these situations, we need to understand what Scripture says about a particular situation to determine what is morally right.

So let's go back to the example of the ventilator. It may look easy to unplug a life support, but Scripture demands that we examine our judgment through the lens of God's Word. Look closely. Scripture says that life is precious. That suffering people should have every access to God's grace. That love for God and love for others are paramount. That motives are important. That conscience cannot be violated. And so on.

These guidelines and others from Scripture have a powerful bearing on whether we are free to pull the plug. They should guide in every situation, eliminating slipshod ethics and "tragic moral choices."

That's what wisdom is all about—employing knowledge and

experience to judge the soundest course of action. And when my family sought wisdom for Dad's situation, it was helpful to be able to reach for a verse from the shelf of theory and use it in the hospital ward, where our decisions had to be made.

A good word on wisdom is James 1:5–6 (PHILLIPS, italics mine): "If, in the process, any of you does not know how to meet any *particular problem* he has only to ask God . . . and he may be quite sure that the *necessary wisdom* will be given him. But he must ask in sincere faith without secret doubts."

Right there, God supplies almost half the answer for our need. As James says, God promises to give *necessary* wisdom for a *particular* problem—that is, wisdom tailored to the problem at hand. Custom-fitted wisdom is needed for discerning particular living or dying distinctions. And because it involves the life and death of a warm-blooded human being, each distinction is subjective—definitely not objective. Every situation is different; every person is unique.

So when it comes to the "pull the plug" question, don't waste your time looking for rules, three-step plans, and a tidy list of dos and don'ts. My family couldn't superimpose on Dad the experience of other families in that nursing home. In the same way, you can't take my family's decision and overlay it like a template on your family's situation. It doesn't work that way. Even a former Surgeon General, a doctor in the highest medical office in the United States, once wrote regarding the prolonging of life, "There is no way that there can be a set of rules to govern this circumstance. Guidelines perhaps are possible, but not rules."[2]

Yet don't be overwhelmed and throw your hands up in despair. Your process of making personal decisions is as close as your doctor, family, and clergy. Insight for making distinctions can be drawn from the experience of a caring physician, the condition of the dying person, and the input of family and counselors who know the value of life. Historically, life and death decisions have always been made this way. Proverbs 11:14 (ESV) tells us, "In an abundance of counselors there is safety," and wisdom is gathered from a physician who knows the facts, a patient who has expressed his or her wishes, a family who is looking out for their loved one first and foremost, and a pastor who can give godly guidance.

A good relationship between physician, patient, family, and pastor can be the wellspring of wisdom. But underline the word *relationship*. Unfortunately, the care, trust, and confidence that once marked the fraternity between a doctor and a patient—or the bond between a pastor and a family—have been replaced by changing standards and, for some, near anonymity. It's rare to find families who have been able to build relationships with a physician or pastor. This requires trust, time, and commitment—and none of these are plentiful in today's culture.

But I encourage you to seek out those up-close and personal relationships to help you discern what is best for a dying family member. Perhaps instead of a pastor, another mature Christian leader could give counsel. And if you feel that a physician only relates to you on a paid-for-service basis, it may be time to request a different doctor.

Wisdom in the Life and Death Setting

James 1:5 implies that a lot of wisdom is already revealed. Remember those commands? The obvious dos and don'ts? Life is a good and God-given thing; it is the most fundamental and irreplaceable condition of the human experience. God is the first one who said, "Choose life," so it's always wise to err on the side of preserving life.[3] We should assume that living is preferable to dying. So go ahead and choose those directives that would be "life beneficial" to a person.

But is it wise to prop up a person in the final death throes with more treatments and machines? Of course not. Dying begins when a person rapidly and irreversibly deteriorates. This is a person for whom death is imminent, a person who is beyond reasonable hope of recovery. Such people have a right to not have death postponed.[4]

The line of distinction is not so much between life and death as it is between life and dying. There are pages in medical dictionaries devoted to defining imminent death. But because the people who are "imminently dying" are unique, warm-blooded human beings in unique circumstances, it's impossible to pin down exactly when the process of dying begins. The Patients Rights Council, an educational and research organization that addresses end-of-life issues, says that true imminent death spans a period of days, perhaps hours. However, courts in some states widen the span of imminent death to a matter of weeks, and some say months. That's why a good relationship with your family's doctors is so critical. You need to get as close to the facts as possible.

There's a point, though, when it's futile and even burdensome to go into a full-court press against death, using every last bit of high-tech, heroic treatment available. We can lean again on the wisdom of Dr. Koop:

> If someone is dying and there is no doubt about that, and you believe as I do that there is a difference between giving a person all the life to which he is entitled as opposed to prolonging the act of dying, then you might come to a time when you say this person can take certain amounts of fluid by mouth and we're not going to continue this intravenous solution because he is on the way out.[5]

This is what "death with dignity" is supposed to be all about.

Okay, so it's possible to gain wisdom about life and dying distinctions. Now what do we do with that wisdom? James 1:5 goes so far as to warn us against asking for wisdom while holding on to secret doubts. It is over this point that so many people stumble.

God demands that we examine our motives. Some people may secretly want a loved one to die to relieve the family's suffering or out of economic considerations or misplaced sympathy or perhaps even out of convenience for the caregivers or society. Think back to what I said in chapter 3. Whether an action qualifies as euthanasia centers on one word: *motive.* If family members insist that IVs and tubes be withheld or withdrawn because "Dad's best years are being wasted taking care of Mother," or "They left that nest egg for us, not for paying hospital bills," then secret doubts can take precedence over God's wisdom.

What about Life-Support Systems?

The death of my father taught my family about finding wisdom in helping my dad live and in letting him die. Giving food to the hungry and water to the thirsty is a requirement of basic decency. And even when it was clear that my father had entered the irrevocable process of death, we wanted to make him as comfortable as possible. This is part of the revealed wisdom of God that mandates compassionate care. It's one of those scriptural dos.

However, doctors advised my family that there are situations where giving food or water, whether by mouth or by tube feeding, is futile and excessively burdensome. Rita Marker of the Patients Rights Council writes, "Patients who are very close to death may be in such a condition that fluids would cause a great deal of discomfort or may not be assimilated. Food may not be digested as the body begins 'shutting down' during the dying process. There comes a time when a person is *truly* imminently dying."[6]

The Christian Medical and Dental Associations affirms that "in exceptional cases, tube feeding may actually result in increased patient suffering during the dying process."[7]

My father was one example. Had he tolerated better the intravenous tube, had he not been dying, we would have faced a different set of circumstances. But we as a family knew his wants and wishes; we knew the way he would want to die. We had asked ourselves the important questions: Were we certain Dad had begun to actually die? Were our motives pure? Our consciences clear? Did we thoroughly seek the counsel of our doctor and clergy? Were we convinced of God's will in this situation?

And most important, were we sure of Dad's salvation in Jesus Christ?

Yes. Yes, to all those questions. And basic decency was lived out poignantly as Kathy, Jay, and my mother moistened Dad's lips with ice chips and helped him sip juice when he could, and even clear broth when possible.

By the way, had my father needed extensive pain medication, our family and doctors would have done whatever was necessary to make him comfortable. As it was, my father was comfortable without medication, but Proverbs 31:6–7 makes a strong case for strong analgesics: "Let beer be for those who are perishing, wine for those who are in anguish! Let them drink and forget their poverty and remember their misery no more." In the context of Proverbs, strong drink is usually an alluring, deceitful thing, but in these two verses, its anesthetic and analgesic qualities are commendable for those who are dying or "in anguish."

My family made these decisions based on an understanding of

Scripture and my dying father's *situation*. But what about the families of people in comas or persistent vegetative states? What about their artificial life-support systems? What about the medical treatment and basic care of people who have severe disabilities to the point where the line between life and death is drawn by a ventilator?

These are questions that would test even wise King Solomon himself!

The Person with a Disability

The first time Dan Piantine and I bumped wheelchairs, I was taken aback by the severity of his paralysis and his frail, thin body. Dan was not dying; he was simply a young man in his early twenties who had disabilities. Dan was born with a neuromuscular disease and thus never developed good muscles. Some people believed he would be better off dead than disabled. But I was impressed by Dan's love for life, and it troubled me when people implied he was suffering needlessly or that he was imprisoned by his body. Such phrases purport to be compassionate but reveal a fundamental fear that really says, "I'd hate to live like that."

For our brief time together, we forgot about such people. Dan and I laughed and talked about our dreams, our hopes, and God.

The second time I met with Dan, it was on a rainy, windy afternoon as he was resting inside his transparent iron lung. A recent heart attack had forced him to spend more time lying down. As I looked through the plastic cylinder, I could see how scoliosis had severely bent and twisted his body. I positioned my chair so I could watch his face in the mirror above the iron lung; I could also see when the whooshing vacuum caused his small, fragile frame to rise and fall. The rain pattered against the window, and there was a quiet and relaxed feeling inside his room.

"Joni, there was a time when I thought I'd be better off dead. I pondered the thought of removing myself from my life support. Funny thing is, I don't think of my iron lung as a life support because there are no tubes, wires, or nurses needed. And my 'lung' is not what they call extraordinary care—for me, it's ordinary. Just something to help me breathe like, let's say, somebody who has polio."

I knew what Dan was saying. What he was describing was *necessary* wisdom needed for his *particular* situation. What is extraordinary care for some people is plain ordinary care for others. Every person is different, each circumstance unique.

Dan continued talking. "God showed me that the definition of quality of life was wrapped up in carrying out His will for my life. No matter what my situation, God could use me."

"We're two peas in a pod on that one," I laughed. I knew of Dan's intensive efforts to educate his religious denomination on accessibility. His heart was bursting with ideas and vision. His body, however, was slowing down. I thought about his recent heart attack and asked, "Have you thought about dying? How will you face it?"

"I've signed a living will stating that when my condition worsens and I can no longer be kept alive by an iron lung, I refuse to accept treatment in other forms. You see, the only other treatment would be a ventilator requiring a tracheostomy. I've talked with doctors about this, and in assessing my condition," he said as his eyes gestured toward his body, "I feel a ventilator would ultimately end in my death because I have so many physical difficulties. I could write a medical journal on my disease alone!"

He went on. "We've come so far in technology that the absolute of when life ends and death is imminent is no longer black and white. I don't want to be caught in the gray. Hey, I'm not saying I have the right to pull myself off my iron lung this minute any more than to ask a doctor to inject a lethal drug. But when it comes to one day facing the way I'll die . . ."

"You've made a judgment in advance," I quietly said. I wasn't going to debate his decision about using a different kind of ventilator. Dan had obviously talked with his family and his pastor. He'd had many discussions with his doctor. And although I know scores of people with severe disabilities who use trach ventilators and would vehemently argue that Dan should go for the trach, I had to respect his decision.

Why? Because Dan understood Scripture and his situation, and he worked through the process of making this incredibly important decision. I had to respect Dan's choice because . . .

- He was *mentally competent* and by no means suicidal. That means he had the *legal right* to decline treatment.
- His *motive* in refusing the trach was not to hasten his death but to safeguard his best chances for life.
- He conferred with his doctor, was a disability expert, and was *totally informed* about his condition. He weighed the risks.
- He *specifically expressed* his wishes, underscoring that further treatment would be extraordinary and burdensome.
- As a *Christian*, Dan was headed for heaven.

When I left Dan's room that day, it was still gray and windy. My thoughts lingered on Dan's choices, and when I heard of his passing not long afterward, I wondered about the way I would approach death as a quadriplegic. Like Dan, I'm an expert on my disability—spinal cord injury has left me with severe disabilities, but nowhere near to the extent Dan experienced. Knowing my kind of quadriplegia, a trach ventilator would definitely *not* be burdensome if, let's say, it got me through pneumonia. And even if I became permanently dependent on a ventilator as a result of pneumonia, it would not be excessively burdensome or futile treatment. Goodness, a ventilator would provide significant life benefits for me! Not so for Dan, because a ventilator could have caused serious and life-threatening complications.

So if I were to decline a ventilator during a bad bout of pneumonia, it would be the same as committing suicide. Even though we both have lived life with severe disabilities, it's obvious that my circumstances are different from what Dan faced. There are no black-and-white rules that compel us to make the same decision.

Thus the question: When is artificial life support extraordinary and when is it ordinary? Treatment that significantly sustains life in a beneficial way is ordinary; treatment that merely postpones or prolongs the act of dying could be considered extraordinary. When I look at my friends who are on ventilators, dialysis machines, or iron lungs, it's clear that such assistive devices are very ordinary treatment. Ventilators, "lungs," and even catheters for people like me produce significant life benefits in relation to the discomfort and cost.

But a ventilator or a dialysis machine or even extensive, expensive surgery could easily be considered extraordinary or burdensome treatment for someone in different circumstances. Assistive devices in some cases could be uncomfortable, costly, and result in no significant life benefits. It's another one of those subjective distinctions.

I appreciate the example of Dr. C. Everett Koop in this matter. While still in the public eye, he wrote of his end-of-life decisions:

> Right now, I am seventy years old and in excellent health. If my kidneys shut down tomorrow, let's say, after a severe infection, I don't know how long I would want to be on

dialysis. It would be foolish and a waste of resources for me
to have a kidney transplant at my age. I would probably opt
to clean up my affairs, say goodbye to my family, and drift
out in uremia.

The important point is that my wife and I know exactly
how each of us feels about the end of life. This will be crucial
if the time comes to make such a decision and I'm not then
able to do so.[8]

I find it no small irony that Dr. Koop *did* end up dying a
few days after suffering kidney failure. But it didn't happen to
him while he was hale and hearty at seventy. He died twenty-six
years later. What was true for Dr. Koop in his careful end-of-life
decision making played out in his nineties. For doctors to try to
reverse kidney failure for Dr. Koop at ninety-six years of age would
have been heroic and, it seems, intrusive in light of what seemed
obvious: it would be prolonging death. Kidney failure at the age
of ninety-six is a natural part of the body's shutting down in the
process of dying.

The guidelines that steer a person with a disabling condition
through the maze of life and death questions are very much the
same for the person who is terminally ill. A man with HIV/AIDS
or a woman with cancer or a child with cystic fibrosis all may be
at points in their lives where, like Dan experienced, they are living
just fine with ordinary treatment. But, like him, one day they will
find their condition deteriorating. They too will wonder, *My doctors
say I only have several months to live. Is it worth having that major
surgery?* These people will try their best to stay out of the gray areas
of life and death decisions. They will need necessary wisdom for
their particular situations.

They will need the wisdom of James 1:5.

The Person in a Coma or
Decreased Level of Consciousness

Sometimes letters say it all. Like this one from the mother of a boy named Jeremy:

> Dear Joni,
>
>   Our twelve-year-old child, Jeremy, was critically injured in an automobile accident. He lived, but remained in a comatose state—we later learned that Jeremy was in a "locked-in condition," unable to open his eyes or speak. He was well nourished through a feeding tube.
>
>   We didn't think we could communicate with Jeremy. But after two years of hard work, physical therapy, God's grace, and money, one day it happened. When I put a softball under his hand, he very slightly moved his thumb for yes and his little finger for no. Our precious son suffered much during two and a half years, and then the Lord took him home shortly before his fifteenth birthday. God used Jeremy's dark valley to point others to him.
>
> Patty Cabeen

Stories like Jeremy's are baffling. Is he in a coma—a state of permanent unconsciousness or decreased consciousness? Then there's the term "unresponsive wakefulness syndrome" (formerly called "persistent vegetative state"). Add to that the doctor's assessment that Jeremy was in a "locked-in condition." To clear up the confusion, a person in a coma is in a suspended sleep state from which they may or may not awaken. A person with unresponsive wakefulness syndrome (UWS) is awake and has sleep cycles, but almost always cannot interact with those around them. Someone in a minimally conscious state is able to show some awareness of their environment beyond what could be considered reflexive responses. In addition to these more commonly recognized categories, there are also other levels of decreased consciousness. Patty's son, with a slight move of his thumb and little finger, was able to respond to those around him but was otherwise paralyzed. That's why his condition was termed "locked-in."

Jeremy's story is at once inspiring yet sad. He represents thousands who are in permanent or semipermanent comas or who have other disorders of consciousness. Many are said to be hopelessly beyond recovery. Yet there are many levels of consciousness, and recent advances in brain imaging have served to show how little we understand the intricate workings of the human brain. A recent study at the University of Cambridge showed that some "vegetative state" patients not only had the ability to pay attention to certain words, but could follow commands as well. The study suggested that specialized devices in the future might enable these patients to interact with the outside world . . . *amazing*.[9]

Sadly, too many people have been called "vegetables" because of the unfortunate coining of the medical term "vegetative state." When people with disabilities are labeled this way, they are in danger of losing personhood (and all the rights that go with being a person, including the right to life).

These persons in permanent comas or other stages of diminished consciousness are precisely those around whom the right-to-die debate gained momentum. Back in 1992, Dr. William Burke, a professor of neurology at St. Louis University, was quoted as saying, "The persistent vegetative state is being used as the hard case in order to get people used to the idea that there are some in our society whose lives aren't worthwhile, who can be terminated."[10] And his words have been proven true, as the right-to-die movement has moved on to securing this "right" for people who are still active and very much alive. In Canada, death with dignity advocates are aiding a disabled woman's case to change the parameters of the nation's doctor-assisted death law—a law that requires a person's death to be "reasonably foreseeable" to be eligible for medical assistance in dying. Those who oppose "broadening the availability of medically assisted dying when death isn't reasonably foreseeable" argue that it leads to the "devaluation of the lives of people with disabilities."[11]

Simultaneously, individuals who have been diagnosed with a consciousness disorder are routinely misdiagnosed and under-cared-for.

Physician and bioethicist Joseph J. Fins wrote a recent article in the *New York Times* titled "Brain Injury and the Civil Right We Don't Think About." Dr. Fins tells about a young woman named Maggie, who while in college had suffered a complex stroke that involved areas deep in her brain. As a result, she was thought to be in a vegetative state—a state "most of us associate with the right to die movement and the legacies of Karen Ann Quinlan, Nancy Cruzan and Terri Schiavo."[12]

But as it turned out, Maggie wasn't in a vegetative state; she was in a "minimally conscious state" (MCS). Fins writes, "Unlike vegetative patients, those in MCS *are* conscious. They demonstrate intention, attention and memory." In Maggie's case, she was even able to communicate through eye blinks. The problem, as Fins notes, is that "these actions may be rare and intermittent, so when family members who witnessed them share their observations with staff members, they are often attributed to a family's wishful thinking."

In a BreakPoint commentary on this issue, Eric Metaxas writes, "MCS was not formally recognized until 2002, which prompts a disturbing question: How many people whose food and water were withdrawn were conscious of what was happening to them? A study Fins cites suggests that the answer could be 'a lot.' The study 'found that 41 percent of patients with traumatic brain injury . . . and thought to be in the vegetative state were in fact in MCS.'"[13]

We can hardly imagine the pain, the financial crunch, the tears, the trauma, and the heartache the families of these individuals endure. These mothers and fathers, and husbands or wives, are placed in the awkward position of speaking on behalf of the person in a diminished state of consciousness or a coma.

The question is usually this: *Why can't we let this person die?*

It is at this exact point that I firmly put on my hat as a disability advocate. People in comas, with unresponsive wakefulness syndrome, or even in locked-in conditions much like Jeremy's, aren't dying (although Jeremy did eventually die of complications); they have severe disabilities. Sure, underline the word *severe* because some of these people can't swallow, but others can. Some make movements that are intentional, others that are reflexive. Because they are nonverbal, they depend on the sensitive interpretations of their caregivers, just as the mother of a newborn can sense different needs communicated in a whimper. And some even dramatically recover after spending years in a coma or minimally conscious state.

But all things considered, they are disabled. And each person, no matter how severe his or her disabling condition, is entitled to treatment and care. Perhaps their biggest disability is that they are "socially disabled," unable to interact with people around them. They are further socially disabled because public sentiment is most often marshaled against their stressed-out families. But people like Jeremy are still persons. And each one has a soul, a spirit.

I won't take time to elaborate on the right-to-die/right-to-care debate swirling around these people and their parents, husbands, or wives, since others have written exhaustively on it. But there is one perspective about an individual with a diminished consciousness disorder that I rarely hear: The Spirit of God is able to work dramatically in the spirit of such a person, perhaps more so than at any other time in his or her life.

It may appear that nothing is taking place in the life of a man or woman in a coma or minimally conscious state, but my friend John Wessells knows otherwise. For years, John and his wife, Gail, have been in and out of facilities for people with severe brain injuries, with a singular task: to sing worship songs, pray, and read Scripture to people in comas. Remember, the work of God is spiritual activity, often very separate from a person's intellect or even basic brain activity. John has sat alongside people who have lain in bed for years, unable to communicate or make any signs of awareness. Yet he has continued to minister in song, prayer, and Scripture reading. And many of these people have emerged from their sleep, having connected with God in an extraordinary way. John writes:

> At that point . . . I was able to recount story after story of the incredible ways people's lives had been changed. How I'd watched a comatose man tap his foot in perfect time to the song I was playing. How I'd spent time with a young man who later told me he'd become a Christian while in his coma—who had heard every word I'd sung and said to him.[14]

How does that happen? Jesus said that these kinds of revelations are not "revealed to you by flesh and blood, but by my Father in heaven."[15] And God can definitely work in the lives of people who have no intellectual capacity. Just look at the example of John the Baptist. While he was yet in his mother's womb, he leaped for joy. And even at his birth, he was filled with the Holy

Spirit.[16] Obviously, God did not need the baby to be able to process complex thought in order to make Himself known. What a profound thought. God may not require a cognizant mind through which to reveal Himself!

This is good news for people who don't have a high IQ. It's good news for the child or adult who has intellectual disabilities. And this is probably the only, and best, good news for the estimated twenty-five thousand people in this country who are considered to be in a diminished stage of consciousness or a coma. I'm convinced God does not need their brains, whether injured or traumatized, to reveal His truth.

And what happens when that time comes for the person in a coma or with unresponsive wakefulness syndrome to depart this earth? How can a family member rest in the knowledge that their loved one has made that right turn into heaven? As Dr. John Frame, professor of systematic theology and philosophy emeritus of Reformed Theological Seminary, concludes, "You simply commend the person to God's mercy. Can a person be saved by God's grace in the moments of unconsciousness preceding death? Certainly."[17]

Admittedly, a truckload of arguments for pulling the plugs of ventilators or feeding tubes can be stockpiled against the needs of people in comas or diminished stages of consciousness: medical expenses, quality of life, family stress, patient suffering, the precedence of court rulings, and pressure from the public. But it is for these very reasons that we should "stop evaluating . . . by what the world thinks about them or by what they seem to be like on the outside."[18]

Such arguments, convincing as they may be, may dictate that it's reasonable to remove life-support systems—in spite of the fact that to do so would be active euthanasia. Rather, people like Jeremy need to be regarded from a transcendent and eternal view: "So we fix our eyes not on what is seen, but on what is unseen, since what is seen is temporary, but what is unseen is eternal."[19]

That's Fine for Jeremy, But . . .

Let's be honest. Maybe you could never see yourself facing life as Jeremy did. You could never live like that. You have enormous respect for Patty Cabeen and her son, but personally, you just would not want to live in permanent or diminished unconsciousness. You want some kind of control over what happens to you.

For you there is another kind of answer, which we'll talk about in the next chapter.

Questions for Discussion and Reflection
Guidelines, Not Prescriptions

Using the guidelines presented in this chapter, discuss the following scenarios. Be sure to point out which guideline(s) you used in making the decision.

Richard, a strong Christian, is a seventy-six-year-old man who for the last twenty years has dealt with a mild form of diabetes. Lately, his diabetic condition has become aggravated due to changes in his diet and encroaching age. His family has been told that Richard needs to undergo a limb amputation to safeguard his health. His family wants him to proceed with the operation, but Richard does not want to.

As Richard's younger brother, what would you advise? What guidelines would you communicate?

Susan, who is not a Christian, has full-blown AIDS and has contracted several infections whose combined impact has weakened her condition. She has an option of enlisting in a new drug treatment program, but she has become weary of the tireless efforts of her Christian friends to keep her alive. She would like to check herself into a hospice and give up the fight.

If you were Susan's Christian friend, what would you do? What guidelines would you apply?

Harold, an athletic young man, just received news from his doctor that he has lymphoma. This has plummeted him into depression, since he also just went through a divorce. Harold has flat-out told his doctor that he does not want the cancer treated at all.

How would you help Harold if you were the doctor? What guidelines would you use?

Jeannie was affected in her shoulder by polio as a teen. She now is suffering post-polio syndrome and is experiencing difficulty in breathing. Her husband is especially concerned at night when Jeannie is asleep, and he fears she may be suffering from oxygen depletion. She is able to walk and can move her polio-affected arm and shoulder slightly. She's not sure if she wants to walk around the rest of her life with a portable ventilator.

What would you tell Jeannie if you were her best friend? What guidelines would you share?

Your ninety-two-year-old father has suffered a series of strokes and has been bedridden for several years. His condition just took a turn for the worse, and he is not able to swallow. The doctor hooked him up to an IV, but his body seems to be bloated as a result of the fluid. Your main concern is that he be made comfortable.

What should you do? What guidelines would you apply?

* * *

How would you classify someone in a permanent vegetative state? Are they still a person? Read the following statement by Robert Wennberg, a medical ethicist who wrote a book titled *Terminal Choices:*

Those operating within a Christian belief-system may be attracted to the conclusion that death is the total and irreversible loss of the capacity to participate in God's creative and redemptive purposes for human life. For it is reasonable for Christians to believe that it is precisely this capacity which endows human life with its special significance. More specifically, this is the capacity to shape an eternal destiny by means of decision-making and soul-making, requiring as it does, both spiritual agency and spiritual receptivity—all of which presuppose conscious existence (that is, psychic life) and not mere organic functioning (that is, somatic life). Indeed it is reasonable to suppose that human organic life has no value in its own right but receives its significance from the fact that it can make possible and sustain personal consciousness and thereby make possible the capacity to participate in God's creative and redemptive purposes . . . When an individual becomes permanently unconscious, the *person* has passed out of existence, even if biological life continues.[20]

Do you agree with Wennberg's evaluation that a permanently unconscious person has lost personhood? Why or why not?

Chapter 9

KNOWING THE DIFFERENCE ISN'T EASY

You and I make wiser decisions after our hearts spend time in the house of mourning. I tend to make good decisions at funerals and poor ones in restaurants. I have made wise financial decisions while surrounded by starving children, and poor decisions from the suburbs. We need to keep our hearts close to the house of mourning to avoid decisions we will regret.

FRANCIS CHAN

B en Coombs, an estate planner and a friend from my church, pulled up a chair next to my desk, opened his briefcase, and spread before me a four-page form titled "Advance Health Care Directive." It explained how to appoint someone to make health care decisions in the event that I became unable to decide for myself.

My eyes slowly scanned each intimidating page. As I zeroed in on one part of the form, the part that looked a little like a living will, the language seemed especially off-putting.

Under point number four—Statement of Desires—it read, "I want my life to be prolonged, and I want life-sustaining treatment to be provided unless I am in a coma that my doctors reasonably believe to be irreversible. Once my doctors have reasonably concluded that I am in an irreversible coma, I do not want life-sustaining treatment to be provided or continued."

I nervously bit my lip and read the paragraph again. The column next to it went even further. It talked about withholding or withdrawing life-sustaining procedures altogether.

But then I glanced at the third column, which presented a dramatic alternative: "I want my life to be prolonged to the greatest extent possible without any regard to my condition, the chances I have for recovery, or the costs of the procedures."[1]

I squirmed a little in my wheelchair. "Why do I have to make a choice and sign this section?" I asked. "Can't my husband just privately tell the doctors my views on prolonged treatment?" Ben pointed out that the person whom I would legally select to make health care decisions for me—if I were unable to make those decisions for myself—needed to faithfully represent my known wishes.

I looked at the place where I would date, sign, and have the form notarized. "What if I change my mind?"

"You should update this every seven years, Joni. Unfortunately," Ben said as he shrugged his shoulders and flipped over the document, "not many people even know about designating a health care proxy. What few do know it—well, they keep putting it off. Then there are those who never take the time to keep the document up-to-date." He shook his head and paused for a moment. "A lot of headache and heartache could be avoided if people only took time to prepare for the future."

I knew exactly what he meant. I needed to prayerfully and carefully think through health care decisions, especially if, in the future, I became mentally unable to think. The physical setbacks I have suffered forced me to think about the way I wanted to approach my own process of dying. Not everyone has that reminder, though.

Questions to Consider

Before I signed my "Joni Tada" on any dotted line, there were serious questions I had to ask. The first was straight out of Psalm 39: "Show me, LORD, my life's end and the number of my days."

On the one hand, Lord, You say that length of days is a blessing, but on the other hand, there has to be a time to die.[2] This is no decision I can make in a vacuum. It has to involve the Lord and Giver of my life. I need to know what You think about the choices facing me.

It helped that I already had an otherworldly perspective on the process of death. The apostle Paul, who was near death himself, was able to confidently say, "We . . . would prefer to be away from the body and at home with the Lord. So we make it our goal to please him, whether we are at home in the body or away from it."[3] I wanted my decision about the way I would die to meet with His approval, from the time I held a pen in my mouth to scratch "Joni" on the signature line to the last breath I would take on this side of eternity.

My decision also involved more than God and me. There were others to consider. For my family's sake, it was important to leave an advance directive about the sort of death I wanted to face.

Not to sign the document about a health care proxy could place my husband, Ken, in an awkward position, especially if I were to become unconscious or mentally incompetent. If a hospital or the state took issue with Ken's directives about my care, then under the judicial doctrine of "substituted judgment," the court would assume the responsibility of determining my desires regarding medical treatment. Without having documented evidence of my wants and wishes, Ken might end up in a fight with the courts in the midst of grieving my last days.

I also needed to assess my relationship with Ken, my family, my friends, and my associates. How would my choices in dying affect them? Would any of my decisions cause intolerable guilt or stress for my husband? And I needed to cement my relationship with my medical care team. Did we both appreciate the limitations of my disability? Did I understand all the facts about life-support systems and their help or hindrance to me?

Having thought through these questions and more, I decided to sign the advance care directive—for my family's sake, for my protection, and for God's commendation.

I took the document home for Ken to study. He knew I had wanted to designate him, as well as an alternate proxy, as my health care agents, but we had been putting off the discussion for some time. After dinner, Ken opened the folder on the kitchen table and slowly read each section. He was quiet, and I wondered what he was thinking.

Much later in the evening, he came into the bedroom and sat on the edge of our bed. "This is a good thing to do," he said with a sigh. "A little difficult to talk about, but a good thing." He looked straight at me and said, "Well, what have you decided?"

"I know my body better than anybody," I said, "and I know that all these decades of paralysis have taken their toll. Let's say when I'm a little older, I face heart failure or need to have a kidney removed or maybe go on dialysis. Quadriplegia has already caused poor circulation and has put my kidneys in jeopardy, so I just don't think it would be worth the risk. I'd probably opt not to have major surgery. Do you see what I mean?"

Ken nodded.

"Plus, I was reading in the Bible the other day about receiving a new body when I get to heaven. That alone makes me not afraid of death," I said. "Like it says, 'And we eagerly await a Savior . . . the Lord Jesus Christ, who . . . will transform our lowly bodies so that they will be like his glorious body.'"[4]

"You sound like a walking theology textbook," he said.

"I've been paralyzed for a long time," I said with a smile. "I'm excited about getting a body that works. Anyway, like I mentioned, I'm not afraid of death, but with things so high-tech and with hospitals so . . . so mechanistic, I'm a little afraid of the way I could die."

"And this is why you want us to sign this," Ken said as he tapped the document in his hand. I nodded, and we both sat there for a long moment. For the rest of the evening, we discussed our wants and wishes of "in sickness and in health . . . till death do us part."

Since that talk took place many years ago, Ken and I have followed our friend Ben's advice and revisited this topic as the years have passed—especially following my diagnosis of stage 3 cancer. For one thing, before I could be admitted, our community hospital *required* us to hand over my advance care directive for their files. Hospitals today are more proactive about such things; they obviously do not want to find themselves in a legal battle should medical decisions be made that are not in accord with the patient's wishes.

And as I shared in chapter 5, in the years leading up to my diagnosis of breast cancer, my struggle with pain stole so much joy and hope. I found myself wondering if some illness might come my way that would put an end to my chronic pain. However, in the face of my diagnosis, I changed my mind about not opting for any major surgery. And once I underwent my mastectomy and began to heal, I discovered a renewed joy for living. I wanted to *live*. I was willing to undergo chemotherapy and radiation if my doctors thought it best. I think this was partly due to my deepening relationships with friends, my sisters, and my husband, Ken. Relationships became so much more precious.

Also, simple pleasures became treasures, such as watching hummingbirds flit through the air or sitting with Ken by the sliding glass door and watching a rainstorm. Life meant so much more—much more than the inconvenience of pain. The point? We never know how highly we value life—how much we're willing to fight for it—until we feel it to be fleeting. So don't be too quick to finalize your preferences, and don't be afraid to return to your directive to reconsider if you've changed your mind.

A Living Will versus an Advance Care Directive

But back to the technical side of this question. Why would I choose an advance care directive with this provision for a health care proxy? Why not simply sign a living will? At first glance, the living will sounds good. You're able to write down on paper exactly how "extraordinary" you want extraordinary medical treatment to be. But living wills have problems.

First, a living will can send a signal that you don't want to have anything done. For instance, in a crowded emergency room, the overworked doctors on duty could interpret a living will to mean that you do not want to be resuscitated, period. Your stretcher is shoved against a wall while other emergencies waiting in line are ushered in.

Second, a living will can't be erased at the last minute. You have no idea when you write it what sort of death you will face or what sort of new treatments may have become available. There's simply no way to accurately foresee the details. And who knows, you may, like most people, want to change your mind when faced with the reality of your own death.

People tend to think a living will gives them control over the way they will die. But in fact, when you sign a living will, you give up rights and control to any doctor who happens to be on the scene to decipher it. There's no guarantee your favorite friendly physician will be the one interpreting the vague wording of a living will.

"But," I hear you saying, "can't my family member explain to the doctor what I meant?"

True, family members can take a stab at deciphering what you meant and explaining it to the physicians on the scene, but the doctor doesn't have to heed the advice. The law gives complete power and protection to the physician who has the document in his or her hands. If it's your own doctor, there may not be a problem, but the way medical facilities are set up makes it unlikely that your physician will be on hand when you sustain a serious injury or illness.

So which is it? Living wills or an advance care directive with a designated proxy? It boils down to this: Do you want to be represented by a piece of paper or a person?

I want a person to speak for me. A person, unlike a living will, is flexible and can be responsive to the circumstances. A person can hire or fire a doctor or even discharge a patient from a hospital. But that individual had better know my exact wishes inside and out—my life will be in his or her hands! Of course, that brings me back to Ken and the advance care directive. I trust Ken. We share the same beliefs, and he knows me better than anybody. I want him to speak for me.

To be honest, neither living wills nor designated health proxies are perfect answers to the dilemma of dying, but of the two, the designated health proxy holds sway. Yet even appointing a person to make medical treatment decisions has its built-in problems. Laws vary all over the nation. One state excludes food and fluids from the category of life-sustaining procedures, and other states allow people to decide specifically whether or not they want food and water withheld.

What's the best thing to do? Ask questions. Whether in a family conference with the ethics committee at the hospital, in a consultation with an estate attorney, or in a discussion with nurses and social workers, it's always good to ask.

The "Miranda" Law: You Have the Right to . . .

Actually, the Patient Self-Determination Act now requires hospitals or nursing homes that receive Medicare or Medicaid funds to explain which documents are recognized in your state, whether living wills or advance care directives. Your rights as a patient are recited to you when you check into a hospital, a kind of detailed briefing like the Miranda warning that law officers give.

So whether you're going in for major heart surgery or just overnight observation, you will be handed a frank written reminder of your right to refuse medical care should your condition become hopeless.

The law was originally drafted in response to the emotional and heartbreaking court proceedings over whether or not to withdraw life support, including food and water, from Nancy Cruzan, a young woman left in a comatose state after a terrible accident. The hope is that this Miranda-like law will make it far more likely that such problems will be resolved at the patient's bedside rather than in some distant courtroom. Before her accident, Nancy had never written down her wishes about the way she would want to die. Her parents were left to argue with the hospital, in and out of the court system, about the appropriate course of action. That's why there was so much controversy when her feeding tube was removed, not to mention the outrage that a young disabled woman was then starved to death.

In one sense, the Patient Self-Determination Act is helpful, because people need to know the facts. Yet in another sense, it's alarming, even frightening. Just having a nurse confront you about your advance care directives and then hand you a sheet spelling out your rights as you check into a hospital for even a minor procedure can be disconcerting. A question like that may affect your judgment about medical treatment, especially if you're depressed about being hospitalized. You wouldn't have any chance to think, pray, or plan wisely!

However, the Patient Self-Determination Act, for all of its flaws, is an attempt to get people thinking about health care proxies and living wills *before* illness strikes and rational thinking goes out the window.

So don't wait until you've arrived at an ER or checked into a hospital. Prayer is the key to preparing yourself and your family for your decision. Ask God to give you the necessary wisdom to make these important choices. Meet with your pastor. Talk with your spouse or parent. Find out from your doctor what directives are legal in your state, or ask your local hospital or senior citizens center to send you information. If you wish, you can visit the website of the National Right to Life and download their document "Will to Live" specific to your state.[5] Then don't put off filling it out!

When You Sign on the Dotted Line

Okay. So I put my signature to a document. What about you?

Remember, an advance care directive is not only a legal directive but also a moral directive. I'd advise you to review a couple of key moral issues before predetermining medical treatment.

If you were my personal friend and I knew you were about to hammer in concrete "No life supports in case of emergency," I would say, "Wait! What if you only need those life supports for a few days? What if then you'd be fine? Don't risk throwing your life away!" One more thing. If you exercised your right to predetermine "no life supports, including feeding tubes," you may end up asking that you be starved to death, a decision for which you would be held morally responsible before God.

A Good Death

If anyone ever died "right," it was Kelly, my five-year-old niece. The youngest of three children, she was the typical tomboy on the family farm. Her mother, Linda, a hardworking single parent, had given her children a lot of responsibilities around the house and barn, and Kelly had become a strong, resourceful, and independent little girl.

One day Granddad noticed that Kelly was limping up the dirt road, slightly dragging her foot. My sister Linda took her to the hospital, and in the course of testing, doctors discovered an enormous cancerous brain tumor. We were shocked and stunned. Surgery could only do so much, and within a month, Kelly could only get around with the help of a wheelchair. After Kelly endured a long hospital stay, the doctors suggested we take her home to die.

Now there were two sets of wheels around the dinner table,

my adult-sized wheelchair and Kelly's miniature one. The entire family rallied to focus love and attention on Kelly as she grew weaker. Everyone tried to make her as comfortable as possible. As a result, it was amazing to see the change in this little girl—not so much the physical change, but the change in her spirit and attitude. No longer the stiff-lipped "I don't need help; I can do it myself" tomboy, she softened into the sweetest, happiest child we've ever known. She virtually memorized "Goldilocks and the Three Bears," wore out her cousin Kay with lots of tea parties, and, most of all, let her imagination run wild when it came to talking about heaven.

Kelly tired easily during those last few months and spent more and more time in bed. She seemed to have no fear of the dark, her disability, or death. One night, I remember passing her dark bedroom and hearing her sing in a half-whisper, "Jesus loves me, this I know . . ."

Kelly taught us a lot about dying right. She talked glowingly of when she would eat ice cream cones with Jesus. She would ride bigger ponies, pour all the ketchup she wanted on her hamburgers, and maybe even talk to bears like Goldilocks. At one point when we were alone in her room, I looked at her in all seriousness and asked, "Kelly, when you see Jesus, will you please tell Him that I said hi? You won't forget?"

She smiled and nodded.

Earlier in the evening on the night Kelly died, she said to her mother, "Mommy, I want to go home."

"But you are home, honey," my sister tenderly told her.

"No, I want to go home with Jesus," she whispered hoarsely. Within several hours, she was there. Kelly passed away in her bed, surrounded by her family, stuffed animals, and a suitcase packed with her jeans, dresses, and toys. Kelly died right, and that fact alone did more to ease the heartache and pain of her passing than anything else.

Hospice Care

Three simple things our family did made Kelly's death good. First, her pain was kept under control, and she was made as comfortable as possible. Second, Kelly's illness brought the family together. Kelly gave sisters, cousins, uncles, and grandparents a reason to unite with, support, and care for one another. Third, Kelly remained a part of the community. Neighborhood children played games at her bedside, Granddad endlessly read picture books to her, and harmony rang out as she weakly joined in family sing-alongs. She was in almost constant contact with loving people who continually convinced her she was not alone or deserted in her time of need.

What happened in Kelly's case is very much what happens in a hospice setting. We practiced most of the principles of hospice care, even though she died before the hospice movement gained traction in the United States. Hospice consists of palliative care for the terminally ill, as well as emotional—and sometimes spiritual— care for the entire family. But a good hospice is not in the business of dying, but of living right up to the end. Most individuals in hospice receive care at home or in a long-term nursing facility they've called home. In recent years, there has been a steady increase of institutional hospice settings, but there's nothing institutional about rooms that are filled with homey furniture, throw rugs, and paintings on the walls. You may even see someone's family pet ambling down the hallway. But the movement needs help.

It's unfortunate that so much attention and so many resources are funneled into legalizing euthanasia while the hospice movement struggles to meet increasing demands. Between 2000 and 2012, the number of patients served by hospice grew by 58 percent, yet during those same years, the number of providers grew by only 39 percent.[6] As you can imagine, lack of providers can lead to less than quality care. Yet studies show that patients who are referred to hospice care sooner rather than later receive better overall care. They live longer, have a better quality of life during their last days, suffer less depression, and, for some populations, have care costs that are less than the costs for those not in hospice.[7] This is especially important to note, as nearly 90 percent of hospice care in the United States is paid for through Medicare, and nearly half of US deaths transpired while the individual was under hospice care.[8]

In this climate of examining medical health costs and government spending, those statistics cannot be ignored. We would communicate a far more compassionate message to those who are terminally ill and dying—and to be honest, even to those for whom dying is a long way off—if we focused our energies on helping people die right.

To die right. That's what it's all about. Unfortunately, euthanasia has become a popular topic because people are led to believe that death by suicide or homicide is more dignified than dying naturally. True, bad medical treatment could be administered at the end of a person's life, but that is true of medically assisted deaths too. What is not true of physician-assisted suicide, however, are the good treatments, the long-practiced mercy symbolized in hospice care. It's the answer for those who fear a death devoid of dignity as the result of bad medical treatment.

We *can* help debilitated or terminally ill people live right. We can alleviate the hopelessness that drives debilitated people to despair by advocating attendant or respite care for stressed-out families. We can support the family with counseling, regular visits, or financial aid. Living in the shadow of dying can be a lonely, desperate time for a person who is severely incapacitated or terminally ill. Our society, especially those who fear God, cannot cringe at the misery that needs mercy or shun the burden that requires bearing. We must be the Lord's hands and heart to those who hurt.

Oh to Be a Burden

Yes, you may think, *that's easy for you to say.*

And it *is* easy for me to say. As a quadriplegic, I have been on the receiving end of other people's help for many years. My caregivers and my husband are experts in giving, even when it hurts, and often they are bone-tired. Part of me feels guilty about that. But God designed my disability to make me not independent, but interdependent. And so, as the recipient of my husband's love, I do absolutely everything I can to support him and my other caregivers with gratitude, as well as to pray for them in their weariness. I also look for ways I can lessen their load. It's the least I can do. It's the *family* thing to do.

We tend to forget this—especially as we grow older or a family member ages or sustains a life-altering disability. Yet this is what families were designed for—especially Christian families. The Christian family showcases to the world that sacrificial service is normal service. Followers of Christ are supposed to give, even when it hurts. We serve, even when—and *especially* when—we're weary or discouraged. Christ calls us to look out for others' interests before our own. And if we *do* feel put-upon, then we find our example in Christ, who "learned obedience from what he suffered" (Hebrews 5:8).

An elderly parent or a mother who receives a diagnosis of multiple sclerosis may be quick to say, "I don't want to be a burden to my family, and I will do everything I can to see that I'm not!" They assume they are doing their family members a Christian service, as if it were their duty not to have to depend on anyone for help.

Gilbert Meilaender wrote in *First Things*, "Families would not have the significance they do for us if they did not, in fact, give us a claim upon each other. At least in this sphere of life we do not come together as autonomous individuals freely contracting with each other. We simply find ourselves thrown together and asked to share the burdens of life while learning to care for each other."[9]

I have many friends with disabilities who have opted to go into a nursing home to spare their families the weight of caring for their needs. They don't want to be a burden. When this thinking becomes the norm, we stop living in the kind of moral community that deserves to be called a family.

A Dying Breath

No matter how we plan for it, death is still the last outrage. But we can make dying as peaceful and serene as possible. You actually can go through death in peace, even serenity. It all depends on the way you view life.

If you believe your earthly life will continue uninterrupted, then you will never be prepared for your final passage, no matter how many documents you sign.

If you believe life has no meaning beyond what you're doing today, then death will be to you an ugly intrusion full of bitterness.

If you believe life is a tiresome struggle weighted with failures and disappointments, then dying may be for you a fatal escape.

But if you accept life as a gift from God, then dying is a part of the given. You can prepare for it. You can approach it. Because you can say with confidence, "For to me, to live is Christ and to die is gain."[10]

Questions for Discussion and Reflection
Be Prepared

Given what you've read in this book and have heard in the media, what steps will you take in the future to be prepared? Think about why you would or wouldn't choose a particular step.

- Have a family meeting.
- Write down your wants and wishes on a notepad and give it to your spouse. It'll suffice.
- Sign an advance care directive with a provision for a health care proxy.
- Review your advance care directive every year and make sure it's up-to-date.
- Wait a while to see what happens in the courts.

The role of health care proxy carries with it great responsibility and doesn't always solve the dilemma. Consider the following scenario:

Mary, a Christian nurse, signed an advance care directive with a provision for a health care proxy while attending a seminar about advance directives. In it, she expressed that she did not want to go on long-term life supports should she become mentally incompetent. Her husband agreed to be her health care proxy. As a result of a serious automobile accident, Mary is now in a coma.

Her husband now must make the decision whether or not to withdraw his wife from life supports.

Should he or shouldn't he ask to have Mary's life supports removed?

Not every situation will have a piece of paper providing some kind of direction. Consider this scenario:

George, an adult with Down syndrome, has been attending your church. He has developed many friends at church. He lives in a residential facility, and his legal guardians are distant relatives who reside in another area of town. George recently developed a degenerative hip problem that, if not corrected, will result in an inability to walk. The director of his residential facility approaches you, concerned that George's legal guardians have vehemently opposed the operation.

To what extent should you get involved in this decision about George's treatment?

Chapter 10

LIFE WORTH LIVING

With Jesus, even in our darkest moments, the best
remains . . . and the very best is yet to be.
CORRIE TEN BOOM

To Whom It May Concern:

I hate my life. You can't imagine the ache of wanting to end your life and not being able to because you're a quadriplegic and can't use your hands.

After the doctors did surgery on my neck, I refused to wear a neck collar. I hate it too. Nobody understands, and nobody will listen to me when I tell them I don't want to live. People feel sorry for me, and I can't stand it. I can't even go to the bathroom by myself.

I don't have the energy to cope. I don't have the strength to face the next day. I want out.

A depressed teen

What would you say to this teen? What sort of advice would you give her? Now that you've come this far, I certainly hope you would not suggest she consider ending her life prematurely!

It's safe to say you want to help. But how much time and support are you willing to invest in her? It would take a lot of effort to sit by her hospital bedside and listen, to hold her hand and genuinely care. She might spit abuse at you; she might turn her head on the pillow and sullenly ignore you; she might even scream orders to a nurse to kick you out of her room.

Could you, with supernatural love, turn the other cheek? Would you be able to care with no strings attached? Would you decide to come back the next day with a magazine and a package of Oreos and just quietly sit at her bedside to watch whatever TV show is blaring on the wall?

That girl is one of millions—depressed, disillusioned, and crying out the unspoken question: *Where is life that is worth living?* Remember, the answer to that question comes not in the form of legal pronouncements, but in people.

Finding Answers in People

The suicidal teen who wrote the "To Whom It May Concern" letter? I know her story well. She begged her friend Jackie to bring from home her mother's sleeping pills or her father's razors. She daydreamed of the time when she could sit up in a motorized wheelchair and power it off a high curb. (*Just my luck*, she thought, *I would only sustain a brain injury and worsen my misery!*) When her friend Jackie stubbornly refused to cooperate, she waited at night until no nurses were around so she could thrash her head on the pillow, hoping her neck would snap at a higher level and cut off her breathing.

I know this teen's story so well because that suicidal girl was me. When a diving accident paralyzed my body, that's not all that became paralyzed. All I wanted was to escape. To escape into daydreams. To escape into sleep. To escape into television. And if I had been able, to escape into death.

I had no pride when it came to bowing out of life. Ironically, at one time I had said, "People who cut their lives short are weak-minded, weak-willed wimps who have spaghetti for a backbone. Why can't they pull themselves up by their bootstraps, hold their breath, and just charge through the suffering without a lot of mopey complaining!" That's how I felt . . . until *I* was the one who became emotional spaghetti.

I am not the only one. Millions more don't want to suffer through anything, whether it be bad health, bad finances, bad pain, or bad relationships. Escape has become the great American pastime, and our culture doesn't help. Our media-oriented society tries to sell us one image after another of the good life free of pain and struggle. When a society buys into that culture of comfort, the lie that suffering does not have purpose takes root in homes, hospitals, and nursing home lounges where life and death decisions are made.

Thankfully, I never was able to engineer that final escape.

Instead I found better answers than an escape hatch. Those answers came in the form of people who loved me. Mrs. Miller, the mother of a high school classmate, visited my bedside once a week. I was embarrassed to show anger in front of her, and besides, she brought home-baked sugar cookies. A boisterous and hardy high school friend named Diana gave up a semester of college to stick by my bedside. Her commitment impressed me, and I liked her corny jokes. A boy named Steve loved the challenge of answering my questions about the Bible. I tolerated him because he was younger than me.

People like these took away my desperate urge to escape. In fact, I found their company much more satisfying than any early exit I could have orchestrated. Steve, for instance, was so caring and persistent. I'll never forget the time I cornered him and whispered, half-crying, "It's so . . . hard."

He didn't say a word, but picked up his guitar and sang an Elton John tune, "Your Song"—"My gift is my song and this one's for you." The words of the song contained no answers whatsoever for my despair, but the tender and innocent expression of compassionate love on his young face was all the healing I needed, at least for that moment.

Mrs. Miller, Diana, Steve, my sisters—these people connected me from one healing moment to the next until I finally surfaced out of my suicidal despair. I looked back into the fog of that funereal depression and realized that I hadn't found answers so much as I had found friends.

God Understands

There's hardly a soul who has ever lived who hasn't wrestled with the overwhelming urge to escape suffering permanently. In fact, the strongest, most stalwart saints are sometimes the most likely candidates for ending it all.

Even a powerful prophet like Elijah discovered he had spaghetti for a backbone. When the wicked queen Jezebel heard through the grapevine that Elijah had wiped out hundreds of her prophets, she went after his neck. Elijah got weak-kneed and ran for his life. When he reached the desert, he gave up. He didn't even have the courage to do himself in—he begged God to perform the mercy killing on him: "'I have had enough, LORD,' he said. 'Take my life.'"[1]

Here's a curious footnote. God had used Elijah to perform spectacular miracles just the day before. He had announced the end of a drought. He was the people's best friend. Elijah had nothing to complain about. Why in the world would he of all people want such a permanent solution for such a little bit of depression?

But that's the point. It doesn't matter whether you are terminally ill and on your last legs or hunch-shouldered with a bad case of the Monday morning blues. Whether you are a grandmother facing a dead end in a nursing home or a young man with cerebral palsy facing a similar end at the bottom of a bottle of pills. From super saints to quads like me, no one is immune.

Elijah would understand. More important, *God understands*. Circumstances may vary from human to human, but we can draw comfort from the fact that all of us are as vulnerable as Elijah. If you look closely at how this mighty prophet surfaced out of his suicidal despair, you'll also see that answers came to him in the form of people. Actually, a Person.

God Himself ministered to the prophet. God handed him food, maybe even something as tasty as Oreos. God gave him sleep, and I'm sure Elijah's rest was as quieting and soothing as Steve's gentle song. God even offered a listening, empathetic ear. The record shows that the angel of the Lord touched Elijah and agreed that "the journey is too much for you."[2] He then presented Elijah with new work to do, and sometimes switching focus onto others is just what the doctor ordered.

How can I help you see? The lesson of Elijah is for all of us. Just as surely as the angel of the Lord personally gave the prophet a sip of cool water and laid him down to rest, the Lord touches our lives through the people He places around us. Mrs. Miller, Diana, Steve, my mother, and my sisters certainly were the hands and heart of God to me. And if there is no Steve or Diana, God can personally come through for you, giving you strength out of nowhere.

Elijah was able to turn the corner and get back on track, thanks to God. I also knew I had turned the corner out of despair when I stopped wrenching my neck on the pillow and started to pray.

My prayer during those midnight moments when the faint fragrance of friendship from my sisters, Diana, and the rest was still in the air? *God, if I can't die, show me how to live.*

Life Is Worth Living with the Person, Jesus Christ

A prayer like "show me how to live" assumes you can see at least a few steps in front of you. But sometimes you can't see a blessed thing. As we read in Isaiah 50:10 (LB), "If such men walk in darkness, without one ray of light . . ."

That pretty much described Dorothy Dalenberg. Total blackness. No way out. Darkness so thick that there wasn't a single ray of light. Dorothy isn't in a coma, doesn't live in a wheelchair, and isn't facing a terminal illness. But her black and burdensome circumstances are the sort most people can identify with—maybe even you.

> Dear Joni,
>
> I injured my neck, which resulted in chronic pain and terrible headaches. Suddenly activities I took for granted came at the price of pain, tears, and frustration. Pushing a grocery cart put my neck in spasms. Cleaning the sink left me in bed with pain pills. I was frequently incapacitated, often going to the emergency room for pain shots.

As I fought to cope, my world unraveled. I had sinus surgery, totaled my car, and was told I have fibromyalgia and a glandular disease. God seemed so distant. I could not feel the peace He promised.

I became very depressed. I wasn't living. I was existing from pain pill to pain pill. No hope. So tired. Gradually I decided life was not worth living.

I began to think of how I would end it all. I felt my family would be better off without me, but I hung on to their love . . . or maybe their love hung on to me.

I didn't see it at first, but God was there all along. In the friends who listened to me, cared for, and accepted me. Through the care of my doctors and a Christian counselor, I learned to control my pain, not let it control me. I discovered my worth is not dependent on what I can do or how I feel. My security comes from who I am in Christ.

My life will never be the same. But God has given me a burden to reach out to others in life's dark hours. Pain I will always have, but now I know He will never leave me or forsake me.

Dorothy Dalenberg

Somewhere in her darkest moment, Dorothy uttered a prayer not unlike my "show me how to live." And Isaiah 50:10 (LB) was handcrafted for people like her and me: "If such men walk in darkness, without one ray of light . . ." She felt the thick blackness, and she knew there was not a single ray of light anywhere. Some would say that's a good signal to end it all. But read the rest of the verse (italics mine): "If such men walk in darkness, without one ray of light, *let them trust the Lord, let them rely upon their God.*"

When Dorothy reached out in the blackness, not expecting

to find a thing—not even a light switch to shed some hope on her bleak circumstances—she found the hand of Someone right in the midst of her darkest hour. God showed her how to live when He showed her *Himself.*

You will only find life worth living if you reach out in the darkness to discover the hand of Christ. Maybe that's why Jesus said, "I am the light of the world." Rays of light are first and foremost found in Him. And listen to what Jesus says not only about light, but about life. He says, "Do not worry about your life," and "I have come that [you] may have life, and have it to the full." He also says, "I am the resurrection and the life," and "I am the way and the truth and the life." Even one of His disciples said, "Lord, to whom shall we go? You have the words of eternal life."[3]

Life is intricately and intimately linked with Jesus. In fact, Jesus is life—He said so Himself. So when we look for life worth living, we must not look for it in happy or heartbreaking circumstances, health, or even relationships. Life is in Christ. That's why Dorothy, and countless others I've mentioned, believe life is worth living. They count the courage and love, friends and smiles, patience and perseverance, poems and music, peace and hope—they count all of this as *life* that God gives, life that is worth the pain.

Back to the Beginning

Remember at the start of this book I told you about my three-week stint in bed with pressure sores? How I described the bird feeder my husband, Ken, hung outside our bedroom window, and the many sparrows that came and visited? I told you how my depression made me envious of the sparrows flying and fluttering so carefree.

During one of those long, dreary evenings in bed, I was reading my Bible and came across the little lecture Jesus gave on sparrows. He was speaking to His disciples about the future, and when He sensed fear rising in their hearts, He reassured them, "Are not two sparrows sold for a penny? Yet not one of them will fall to the ground outside your Father's care. And even the very hairs of your head are all numbered. So don't be afraid; you are worth more than many sparrows."[4]

I glanced at the bird feeder and smiled. I could understand Jesus noticing an eagle or a falcon or a hawk falling to the ground. Those are important birds created by God—the kind worth attending to. But a scrappy sparrow? They're a dime a dozen. Jesus said so Himself.

Yet from thousands of bird species, the Lord chose the most insignificant, least-noticed, scruffiest bird of all. A pint-sized thing that even dedicated birdwatchers ignore.

That thought alone calmed my fears. I felt significant and noticed. Because if God takes note of each humble sparrow—who it is, where it is, and what it's doing—I know He keeps tabs on me. For my remaining days in bed, every bird that visited the feeder served as a joyful reminder of God's concern for every detail of my life.

As I told you in the first chapter, my pressure sores healed. In the twenty-five years since that summer, I've also faced chronic pain and stage 3 breast cancer. I'm writing this on the other side of fifty years in a wheelchair. *Fifty years.* And yet there will inevitably be days when I'll still face fear. Worries will press in. Doubts will assault. Depression will lay me low. And you don't have to be in a wheelchair to identify.

We both will do well to remember this: "Do not be afraid, little flock, for your Father has been pleased to give you the kingdom."[5] If the great God of heaven concerns Himself with a ragtag little sparrow clinging to a bird feeder outside my window, He cares about you.

And Forward to the End

One day, your banged-up, bruised body won't matter a whole lot. Right now, it screams for your undivided attention, but if you place your trust in Christ, the day is coming when your suffering body will take a back seat. I once heard someone say, "At present we wear our bodies on the outside and our souls on the inside. But in heaven, we will wear our bodies on the inside and our souls on the outside."

What else could the Bible possibly mean when it says that one day we will be clothed in righteousness? We will wear our righteousness as if it were a beautiful garment. I'm sure that's why the Bible also tells us to get ready on this side of eternity by clothing ourselves "with compassion, kindness, humility, gentleness and patience."[6]

Be patient. Don't give up. This life is not over yet. It will get better. One day, you will enjoy the most perfect final exit, one orchestrated by the Master Designer Himself.

This is how the psalmist speaks of our final destiny in Psalm 49:15:

> But God will redeem me from the realm of the dead;
> he will surely take me to himself.

Questions for Discussion and Reflection
Living Well

How would you summarize the message of this book?

How do you think your church could get involved in the lives of people facing issues relating to life and death? Consider what the church could do for the following:

- someone who is terminally ill
- a family with a loved one in a coma
- a quadriplegic living in a nursing home
- a mom whose twins both have disabilities

Why do you think some people are slow to get involved? What would keep you from trying any of the above ideas you developed?

Apart from involvement in the lives of individuals, what do you think is the role of the church in the societal debate on issues surrounding life and death?

EPILOGUE

*Don't let the world around you squeeze you into its own
mould, but let God remould your minds from within, so
that you may prove in practice that the plan of God for
you is good, meets all his demands and moves towards
the goal of true maturity.*

ROMANS 12:2 PHILLIPS

Subjects that were once taboo in polite conversation—mercy
killing, the latest demands of the LBGTQ movement, and
even "gender reassignment"—are now plastered in the headlines
of popular magazines and websites. What was once off-limits is
now out of the closet, and we have become inured to its shock
value. Formerly unmentionable subjects now quickly find a way
into lunchroom and carpool banter.

Without the absolutes of Scripture, peoples' convictions about
such subjects are fashioned by what seems right in their own eyes.
Paul alluded to this when he wrote to Timothy, "For the time will
come when people will not put up with sound doctrine. Instead,
to suit their own desires, they will gather around them a great
number of teachers to say what their itching ears want to hear"
(2 Timothy 4:3).

And that's what it's all about, isn't it? *Our own desires.* Our willful determinations ("rights") dressed up in politically correct language to give them a veneer of respectability.

That's exactly what happened when physician-assisted suicide elbowed its way into our national dialogue. Something monstrous has become commonplace, blending with casual talk about the weather, football scores, and pop culture. All of its shock value has been drained away.

Left to our own uninformed senses, we quickly default to that which is most comfortable and convenient. Add suffering to that mix, and our society will quickly jettison all other considerations. We seem ready to sacrifice anything to be rid of pain and suffering—including our own lives. It especially hurts that people with disabilities—men and women who have endured much and exhibited great courage—have been charmed and anesthetized by the allure of so-called "death with dignity."

Are we, in fact, being squeezed into the mold of the world around us? *Or are we allowing God to daily remold our minds from within?* Are the constantly evolving opinions and fashions of our contemporary world beginning to shape us—our thoughts, our opinions, our sensibilities? Or are we allowing God's Word to challenge, refute, and replace those sentiments with eternal truths?

Please think about these things, my friend.

How do you reawaken shock value after it's been diluted, rephrased, and painted over with soft pastels? I want people to become alarmed again—yes, aghast by the taking of another's life. Or even our own life.

I think we should save our sharpest outrage for the way assisted suicide has been sanitized, softened, and reinterpreted by our politicians and popular culture. Death has been clothed in a crisp white lab coat and "reasonable, compassionate, progressive" language.

But it is still death.

Death before its time.

It is still wrong.

And it still grieves the Lord of life.

I'm reading in the book of Ezekiel as I pen these words, and seeing again how repugnant the taking of innocent life was to God. The Israelites had been drawn into child sacrifice, offering their babies in the fire to the hideous idol Moloch. It was a religion of convenience that pretty much said, "Here, god, you can have my child . . . as long as I can live the way I want to."

Life isn't always convenient. As I can testify, life can come with a great deal of suffering. But it is still life—a precious gift of the living God. And it is still His call when it begins and when it ends.

Don't let the world—no matter how sweet-tongued and superficially rational it may sound—squeeze you into its own mold.

Molding God's people is God's job. And He does it from the inside out.

A CLASSIC PERSPECTIVE ON THE HIPPOCRATIC OATH

We have recently seen the ambivalent manner in which society deals with physicians who assist patients in committing suicide.

I have always defined euthanasia as "death by someone's choice," someone who considers the life in question no longer worth living. There is a difference between helping a person live all the life he is entitled to and prolonging the act of dying. There is also a difference between letting nature take its course in a dying life and speeding the death of an individual by whatever means and for whatever purposes, no matter how well intended.

Thirty years ago and earlier, the debate about euthanasia centered around pain that could not be relieved. Today, when it is possible, in almost every case, to relieve pain and suffering, the debate has shifted to ending the lives of those despairing of their situation, who don't want to die of their diagnosis, who know they are incurable, or who have lost self-command, dignity, or quality of life.

We have overemphasized curing, compared to caring, to our detriment. The medical tradition that has served us so well for more than two thousand years came from Hippocrates and his disciples. They had very little to offer patients except care and integrity. Among other things, the Hippocratic Oath states, "I will use treatment to help the sick according to my ability and judgment, but I will never use it to injure or wrong them."

The Hippocratic Oath has been the most enduring ethical legacy of the practice of medicine, being passed on from teacher to student, from physician to new physician, from generation to generation. The Hippocratic Oath and the tradition surrounding it became the medical ethics and the value system that made Western medicine the art that it has become. Only recently, since the Second World War, has this noble tradition been threatened. The function of the Oath in today's society is the same as when it was first spoken. The Oath calls physicians to a higher ethical standard than that of society in general.

In the society that produced the Hippocratic Oath, the lines between physician, witch doctor, and magician had become blurred, as had the line between physician and executioner. The laws of the society in which the first Hippocratic physicians took that Oath allowed them to kill, allowed abortion, and allowed them to abuse the privacy of their relations with patients.

The Oath called on physicians not to change the laws of society—that was not their function—but to commit themselves to a higher ethical standard.

The Oath was trying to say, "I [that is, we of the school of Hippocrates] am above such things. Though others who call themselves physicians do these things, I will not. You can count on my being a responsible physician."

You will be well on your way to understanding the Hippocratic tradition when you understand its basic premise: the physician is a healer. Perhaps the most important aspect of the Hippocratic Oath is that it does not at any time or in any way speak of the doctor's role in the relief of human suffering. The ancient doctor of those days could cure practically nothing, and it is self-evident that he did what he could within the framework of "do no harm."

With few medications or procedures in his armamentarium, the ancient physician often succumbed to the temptation to kill, to assist in suicide, and so to alleviate suffering by ending it with death. This, however, was not for Hippocrates. Alleviate suffering, to be sure, but never if it threatened the sanctity of human life, the basic premise of the healing physician.

I went to medical school to learn how to save lives and alleviate suffering. I saw no tension between those points of view, because I was a Hippocratic physician. There was an absolute proscription on the taking of life. If I could heal or cure, I would do it, but in doing that or failing that, I would relieve the suffering of my patient.

Hippocratic medicine does not require that the act of dying ever be prolonged. If my patient has received all that I can do for him, and if healing is not possible, I can alleviate his suffering and still stay well within the bounds of "do no harm."

C. Everett Koop, MD,
United States Surgeon
General (1982–1989)

NOTES

CHAPTER 1: *Painful Words*

1. Joni Eareckson Tada, *Joni: An Unforgettable Story*, 4th ed. (Grand Rapids: Zondervan, 2012), 79–80.
2. Derek Humphry, *Final Exit: The Practicalities of Self-Deliverance and Assisted Suicide for the Dying* (New York: Random House, 1992).
3. *Today Show* transcripts (August 5, 1991).
4. Bonnie Angelo, "Assigning the Blame for a Young Man's Suicide," *Time* (November 18, 1991), 13, http://content.time.com/time/magazine/article/0,9171,974297,00.html (accessed June 15, 2017).
5. "Terminology of Assisted Dying," Death with Dignity, www.deathwithdignity.org/terminology (accessed June 15, 2017).
6. Paul Marx, *And Now . . . Euthanasia*, 2nd ed., Issues in Law and Medicine (Terre Haute, IN: National Legal Center for the Medically Dependent and Disabled, 1985).
7. Sheri Linden, "'Me Before You': Film Review," *Hollywood Reporter* (May 24, 2016), www.hollywoodreporter.com/review/mc-before-you-film-review-896289 (accessed June 15, 2017).
8. Sharon Begley, "Choosing Death," *Newsweek* (August 26, 1991), 43.

CHAPTER 2: *The Pain Is Real*

1. God loves perfectly, no matter what level our spiritual maturity; however, many attest that God reserves special affection for individuals who seek Him and fear Him in the manner of the apostle John or King David, men who enjoyed a "best friend" status with God. My use of Peter Kreeft's quote is to underscore that God is more concerned with who we become than

with what we do, thus giving each of us, no matter what our functioning ability, the opportunity to please God, regardless of our vocation.

2. By tragic moral choices, I mean choices where the option that seems most morally correct directly contradicts another moral directive. In these scenarios, there is seemingly no correct choice, and one fears that the best option is merely the lesser of two evils.

CHAPTER 3: *Why Not Die?*

1. "Suicide Statistics," American Foundation for Suicide Prevention, taken from Centers for Disease Control and Prevention (CDC) Data and Statistics Fatal Injury Report for 2015, https://afsp.org/about-suicide/suicide-statistics (accessed June 15, 2017).

2. "Oregon Death with Dignity Act: Data Summary 2016," Oregon Public Health Division, Center for Health Statistics (February 10, 2017), https://public.health.oregon.gov/ProviderPartnerResources/EvaluationResearch/DeathwithDignityAct/Documents/year19.pdf (accessed June 15, 2017); "Washington State Department of Health 2015 Death with Dignity Act Report: Executive Summary," www.doh.wa.gov/portals/1/Documents/Pubs/422–109-DeathWithDignityAct2015.pdf (accessed June 15, 2017).

3. "Prioritized List of Health Services," Oregon Health Plan, www.oregon.gov/oha/HSD/OHP/Pages/Prioritized-List.aspx (accessed June 15, 2017).

4. "Oregon Death with Dignity Act: 2015 Data Summary," Oregon Public Health Division (February 4, 2016), https://public.health.oregon.gov/ProviderPartnerResources/EvaluationResearch/DeathwithDignityAct/Documents/year18.pdf (accessed June 15, 2017).

5. Isaac Asimov, in an endorsement in Derek Humphry's *Final Exit: The Practicalities of Self-Deliverance and Assisted Suicide for the Dying* (New York: Random House, 1992), i.

6. Bob Smietana, "Most Americans Say Assisted Suicide Is Morally Acceptable," LifeWay Research (December 6, 2016), http://lifewayresearch.com/2016/12/06/most-americans-say-assisted-suicide-is-morally-acceptable (accessed June 15, 2017).

7. Charles Colson, "Keeping Pets in Their Place," *Christianity Today* (April 29, 2008), www.christianitytoday.com/ct/2008/april/35.80.html (accessed June 15, 2017).

8. C. Everett Koop, "Euthanasia: Murder or Mercy?" *Berean League Backgrounder* 2 (March 1987): 1.

9. "Terminology of Assisted Dying," Death with Dignity, www.deathwith dignity.org/terminology (accessed June 15, 2017).

10. Jason Barber, "Dignity in Dying," Death with Dignity (October 2015), www.deathwithdignity.org/stories/jason-barber-dignity-dying (accessed June 15, 2017).

11. See "The Hemlock Maneuver," *Physician Magazine* (March/April 1991), 2.

CHAPTER 4: *Your Decision Matters to Others*

1. See Editors, "Euthanasia: Final Exit, Final Excuse," *First Things* (December 1991), 5.

2. "Oregon Death with Dignity Act: 2015 Data Summary," Oregon Public Health Division (February 4, 2016), https://public.health.oregon.gov/ ProviderPartnerResources/EvaluationResearch/DeathwithDignityAct/ Documents/year18.pdf (accessed June 15, 2017).

3. See Melissa Bailey, "So Long, Hippocrates: Medical Students Choose Their Own Oaths," *STAT* (September 21, 2016), www.statnews.com/2016/09/21/ hippocratic-oath-medical-students-doctors (accessed June 15, 2017).

4. See Kathy Ostrowski, "Doctors Issued DNR Order for Disabled Newborn without Telling His Parents," *LifeNews.com* (April 4, 2016), www.lifenews.com/2017/02/23/doctors-issued-dnr order-for-disabled -newborn-without-telling-his-parents (accessed June 15, 2017).

5. See Peter Daniel Murray, Denise Esserman, and Mark Randolph Mercurio, "In What Circumstances Will a Neonatologist Decide a Patient Is Not a Resuscitation Candidate?" *Journal of Medical Ethics* 42 (March 2016): 429–34, http://jme.bmj.com/content/42/7/429.info (accessed June 15, 2017).

6. Alex Schadenberg, "Euthanasia: Theory and Reality," Euthanasia Prevention Coalition (September 29, 2015), http://alexschadenberg.blogspot .com/2015/09/euthanasia-theory-and-reality.html (accessed June 15, 2017).

7. Susan Donaldson James, "Death Drugs Cause Uproar in Oregon," *ABC News* (August 6, 2008), http://abcnews.go.com/Health/story?id=5517492 &page=1 (accessed June 15, 2017).

8. See "Oregon's Death with Dignity Act—2014," Oregon Public Health Division (February 2, 2015), http://public.health.oregon.gov/

ProviderPartnerResources/EvaluationResearch/DeathwithDignityAct/
Documents/year17.pdf (accessed June 15, 2017).

9. "Life Expectancy for Type 1 Diabetes May Be Improving," *Fox News Health* (January 7, 2015), www.foxnews.com/health/2015/01/07/life
    -expectancy-for-type-1-diabetes-may-be-improving.html (accessed June 15, 2017).

10. See N. Gregory Hamilton, MD, and Catherine Hamilton, MA, "Competing Paradigms of Responding to Assisted-Suicide Requests in Oregon: Case Report," Physicians for Compassionate Care Education Foundation (May 6, 2004), www.pccef.org/articles/art28.htm (accessed June 15, 2017).

11. Eline Gordts, "Marc and Eddy Verbessem, Deaf Belgium Twins, Euthanized after Starting to Turn Blind," *HuffPost* (January 15, 2013), www.huffingtonpost.com/2013/01/14/marc-eddy-verbessem-belgium
    -euthanasia_n_2472320.html (accessed June 15, 2017).

12. See "Success Stories," Helen Keller National Center for Deaf-Blind Youths and Adults, www.helenkeller.org/hknc/success-stories (accessed June 15, 2017).

13. See Philippa Willits, "I Am Disabled and People Tell Me on a Regular Basis That They Would Rather Die Than Be Like Me," *XOJane* (January 30, 2015), www.xojane.com/issues/assissted-suicide-leans
    -towards-helping-non-disabled-people (accessed June 15, 2017).

14. See "Portland Neighborhoods Littered with Hate Letters Targeting Disabled," *Fox 12 Oregon* (September 6, 2013), www.kptv.com/
    story/23089900/flyer-targets-people-with-disabilities-mayors-office
    -says-author (accessed June 15, 2017); Ben Baumberg, Kate Bell, and Declan Gaffney, "Scroungers, Fraudsters and Parasites: How Media Coverage Affects Our View of Benefit Claimants," *New Statesman* (November 20, 2012), www.newstatesman.com/economics/2012/11/
    scroungers-fraudsters-and-parasites-how-media-coverage-affects-our
    -view-benefit-cl (accessed June 15, 2017).

15. "Crime Against Persons with Disabilities, 2009–2014—Statistical Tables," Bureau of Justice Statistics (November 2016), www.bjs.gov/
    content/pub/pdf/capd0914st_sum.pdf (accessed June 15, 2017).

16. Lana Shadwick, "Texas Man Who Hospital Wanted to Kill Has Died," *Breitbart* (December 23, 2015), www.breitbart.com/big-government/

2015/12/23/texas-man-who-hospital-wanted-to-kill-has-died (accessed June 15, 2017).

17. Kaitlin McCulley, "Mom Fights to Save Life of Son on Breathing Machine," *ABC13 Eyewitness News, Houston* (December 4, 2013), http://abc13.com/news/mom-fights-to-save-life-of-son-on-breathing-machine/1110135 (accessed June 15, 2017).

18. "Physician-Assisted Suicide: A Family Struggles with the Question of Whether Mom Is Capable of Choosing to Die," *The Oregonian/Oregon Live* (February 4, 2015), www.oregonlive.com/health/index.ssf/2015/02/physician-assisted_suicide_a_f.html (accessed June 15, 2017).

19. At the time of this writing, the UK has not amended Suicide Act 1961 outlawing assisted suicide; however, ongoing attempts threaten the soundness of this law, especially in light of Justice Eleanor King's blatant disregard for protecting life.

CHAPTER 5: *Your Decision Matters to You*

1. Viktor E. Frankl, *Man's Search for Meaning*, 3rd ed. (New York: Simon & Schuster, 1984), 86–87.

2. Frankl, *Man's Search for Meaning*, 87, 135, italics mine.

3. Idea gleaned from James M. Wall, "In the Face of Death: Rights, Choices, Beliefs," *Christian Century* (August 21–28, 1991).

4. Quoted in Duane Riner, "Quadriplegic Petitions Court to Let Him Die," *Atlanta Constitution* (August 15, 1989), A1, A18.

5. For further insight into Dr. Viktor Frankl's views on God, refer to his book *The Unconscious God* (New York: Simon & Schuster, 1975).

6. Luke 22:42, 44.

7. Associated Press, "Judge Rules Quadriplegic Entitled to End Own Life," *Tulsa World* (September 7, 1989), www.tulsaworld.com/archives/judge-rules-quadriplegic-entitled-to-end-own-life/article_be2547e6-2339-5662-9f10-c4eff0d6d612.html (accessed June 15, 2017).

8. John Donne, "Meditation XVII," in *Devotions upon Emergent Occasions* (1623).

9. Idea gleaned from Erika Schuchardt, *Why Is This Happening to Me? Guidance and Hope for Those Who Suffer* (Minneapolis: Augsburg, 1989).

CHAPTER 6: *Your Decision Matters to the Enemy*

1. Matthew 4:3, 5–6, 9.
2. John 8:44.
3. C. Samuel Storms, *To Love Mercy: Becoming a Person of Compassion, Acceptance, and Forgiveness* (Colorado Springs: NavPress, 1991), 18.
4. Storms, *To Love Mercy*, 32.
5. Viktor E. Frankl, *Man's Search for Meaning*, 3rd ed. (New York: Simon & Schuster, 1984), 100–101.
6. 2 Corinthians 4:8–10 LB.
7. Matthew 18:8.
8. "Deliverance from Hell," *Hemlock Quarterly* 45 (October 1991): 5.
9. Jude 6; 2 Peter 2:4. Without referencing Ezekiel 28:11–19, it is universally held among Christians that the devil is one of the fallen angels mentioned in Jude 6 and 2 Peter 2:4. It's a logical conclusion that the greatest among demons would be Satan.
10. 2 Corinthians 4:4.
11. Revelation 20:7–10.

CHAPTER 7: *Your Decision Matters to God*

1. 2 Samuel 1:9–10 LB.
2. See 1 Chronicles 10:4.
3. The real issue in this story is, indeed, not one of mercy killing, but one of harming the person set apart for the Lord's service. David was angry that the Amalekite chose to "destroy the LORD's anointed" (2 Samuel 1:14). We should certainly have as much respect for the life of a chosen child of God as the Israelites did for their king.
4. Exodus 20:13.
5. See Judges 9:54–57; 2 Samuel 1:9–16; 1 Kings 16:15–19; Matthew 27:5.
6. 1 Corinthians 6:19–20.
7. Mark 15:23.
8. John 19:29.
9. David Mathis, "The Wine Jesus Drank," Desiring God (May 27, 2010), www.desiringgod.org/articles/the-wine-jesus-drank (accessed June 15, 2017).
10. John MacArthur, "A Closer Look at the Cross," Grace to You (March

27, 1988), www.gty.org/library/sermons-library/80-48 (accessed June 15, 2017).

11. For example, Romans 12:9, 17, 21; 1 Thessalonians 5:22; 1 Peter 3:9–12. Some evangelicals believe moral principles can be violated when there is a conflict of duties. However, in Scripture, it is never right to disobey a command of God, and it is never sinful to do right. For further study on whether it is ever right to morally disobey God, see Dr. John Frame's book *Medical Ethics: Principles, Persons, and Problems* (Phillipsburg, NJ: Presbyterian and Reformed, 1988).

12. Norman L. Geisler, *Christian Ethics: Contemporary Issues and Options* (1989; repr., Grand Rapids: Baker, 2010), 175.

13. "Ol' Man River," lyrics by Oscar Hammerstein II; music by Jerome Kern. The song was first performed live in December 1927.

14. Hebrews 2:14–15 LB.

15. 1 Corinthians 15:26.

16. John 10:10 LB.

17. George MacDonald, *A Book of Strife in the Form of the Diary of an Old Soul* (London: Hughes, 1880), 163.

18. See 1 Corinthians 15:53–54; 2 Corinthians 5:2–4.

19. Ephesians 3:10 Phillips.

20. Matthew 6:34.

CHAPTER 8: *Sustaining Life, but Not Prolonging Death*

1. Job 1:21.

2. C. Everett Koop, MD, "Right to Die (II)," in *Human Life Review* 2, no. 2 (Spring 1976): 45.

3. See Deuteronomy 30:19; 2 Kings 18:32.

4. See Christian Medical and Dental Associations, "Euthanasia," CMDA Ethics Statements, https://cmda.org/library/doclib/CMDA-Ethics -Statementsworeferences14.pdf (accessed June 15, 2017); see also "Euthanasia Ethics Statement with References," https://cmda.org/ library/doclib/Euthanasia-with-References.pdf (accessed June 15, 2017).

5. C. Everett Koop, "The Surgeon General on Euthanasia," *Presbyterian Journal* (September 25, 1985), 8.

6. Rita L. Marker, "Advance Directive: Protecting Yourself and Your

Family (Part 2)," Patient Rights Council (December 2006), www
.patientsrightscouncil.org/site/advance-directive-protecting-yourself
-and-your-family-part-two (accessed June 15, 2017).

7. Christian Medical and Dental Associations, "Withholding Nutrition,"
CMDA Ethics Statements, https://cmda.org/library/doclib/CMDA
-Ethics-Statementsworeferences14.pdf (accessed June 15, 2017).

8. C. Everett Koop, "The End Is Not the End," *Christianity Today*
(March 6, 1987), 18, www.christianitytoday.com/ct/1987/march-6/end
-is-not-end.html (accessed June 15, 2017).

9. "Patient in 'Vegetative State' Not Just Aware, but Paying Attention,"
University of Cambridge Research (October 31, 2013), www.cam.ac.uk/
research/news/patient-in-vegetative-state-not-just-aware-but-paying
-attention (accessed June 15, 2017).

10. Callista Gould, "Two Real Life 'Awakenings' Challenge PVS Diagnosis,"
National Right to Life News (January 1992), 34.

11. Nicole Ireland, "Medically Assisted Death Has Been Legal for Almost
a Year, but Another Battle Is Brewing," CBC News (April 20, 2017),
www.cbc.ca/news/health/medically-assisted-dying-court-case-julia-lamb
-1.4067629 (accessed September 13, 2017).

12. Joseph J. Fins, "Brain Injury and the Civil Right We Don't Think About,"
New York Times (August 24, 2017), www.nytimes.com/2017/08/24/opinion/
minimally-conscious-brain-civil-rights.html (accessed September 13, 2017).

13. Eric Metaxas, "BreakPoint: Minimally Conscious, not Minimally
Human," BreakPoint (September 1, 2017), http://breakpoint.org/2017/
09/breakpoint-minimally-conscious-not-minimally-human (accessed
September 13, 2017).

14. John Wessells, *Conversations with the Voiceless: Finding God's Love in Life's
Hardest Questions* (Grand Rapids: Zondervan, 2004), 18.

15. Matthew 16:17.

16. See Luke 1:44–45.

17. Dr. John M. Frame, personal letter.

18. 2 Corinthians 5:16 LB.

19. 2 Corinthians 4:18.

20. Robert N. Wennberg, *Terminal Choices: Euthanasia, Suicide, and the Right
to Die* (Grand Rapids: Eerdmans, 1989), 159.

CHAPTER 9: *Knowing the Difference Isn't Easy*

1. "Durable Power of Attorney for Health Care" (California Civil Code Sections 2410–2443).
2. Ecclesiastes 3:2.
3. 2 Corinthians 5:8–9.
4. Philippians 3:20–21.
5. This can be found at National Right to Life, www.nrlc.org/medethics/willtolive/states (accessed June 15, 2017).
6. "Statistics Every Hospice Administrator Should Know" Total Triage: Blog (April 7, 2015), http://afterhourstriage.com/blog/hospice-nursing/statistics -every-hospice-administrator-should-know (accessed June 15, 2017).
7. Dan Hogan, "Why Hospice Care Is More Important Than Ever Before," National Association for Home Care and Hospice, www.nahc.org/news/why -hospice-is-more-important-today-than-ever-before (accessed June 15, 2017); see also Sarah Friebert and Conrad Williams, "NHPCO's Facts and Figures: Pediatric Palliative and Hospice Care in America, 2015 Edition," National Hospice and Palliative Care Organization, www.nhpco.org/sites/default/files/public/quality/Pediatric_Facts-Figures.pdf (accessed June 15, 2017).
8. See Christopher Hogan, "Spending in the Last Year of Life and the Impact of Hospice on Medicare Outlays (Updated August 2015)," www.medpac.gov/docs/default-source/contractor-reports/spending-in -the-last-year-of-life-and-the-impact-of-hospice-on-medicare-outlays -updated-august-2015-.pdf?sfvrsn=0 (accessed June 15, 2017).
9. Gilbert Meilaender, "I Want to Burden My Loved Ones," *First Things* (March 2010), www.firstthings.com/article/2010/03/i-want-to-burden -my-loved-ones (accessed June 15, 2017).
10. Philippians 1:21.

CHAPTER 10: *Life Worth Living*

1. 1 Kings 19:4.
2. 1 Kings 19:7.
3. John 8:12; Matthew 6:25; John 10:10; 11:25; 14:6; 6:68.
4. Matthew 10:29–31.
5. Luke 12:32.
6. Colossians 3:12.

RESOURCES

FOR FURTHER READING

Cameron, Nigel M de S. *The New Medicine: Life and Death after Hippocrates*. Wheaton, IL: Crossway, 1992.

Dunlop, John. *Finishing Well to the Glory of God: Strategies from a Christian Physician*. Wheaton, IL: Crossway, 2011.

Dyck, Arthur J. *Life's Worth: The Case against Assisted Suicide*. Grand Rapids: Eerdmans, 2002.

Garberding, Virginia. *Please Get to Know Me: Aging with Dignity and Relevance*. Enumclaw, WA: Winepress, 2008.

Geisler, Norman L. *Christian Ethics: Contemporary Issues and Options*. 2nd ed. Grand Rapids: Baker Academic, 2010.

Moll, Rob. *The Art of Dying: Living Fully into the Life to Come*. Downers Grove, IL: InterVarsity, 2010.

Rossi, Melody. *Sharing Christ with the Dying: Bringing Hope to Those Near the End of Life*. Grand Rapids: Baker, 2014.

Stewart, Gary et al. *Basic Questions on End of Life Decisions: How Do We Know What's Right?* Grand Rapids: Kregel, 1998.

Verhey, Allen. *The Christian Art of Dying: Learning from Jesus*. Grand Rapids: Eerdmans, 2011.

RESOURCES FROM JONI AND FRIENDS

Joni and Friends, Inc., and Joni Eareckson Tada. *Beyond Suffering Bible: Where Sufferings Seem Endless, God's Hope Is Infinite.* Carol Stream, IL: Tyndale, 2016.

Tada, Joni Eareckson. *Heaven: Your Real Home.* Grand Rapids: Zondervan, 1995.

Tada, Joni Eareckson, and Nigel M. de S. Cameron. *How to Be a Christian in a Brave New World.* Grand Rapids: Zondervan, 2006.

Tada, Joni Eareckson, and Steven Estes. *When God Weeps: Why Our Sufferings Matter to the Almighty.* Grand Rapids: Zondervan, 1997.

Joni Eareckson Tada is founder and CEO of Joni and Friends, a Christian organization that accelerates Christian outreach in the disability community worldwide. Joni is the author of many best-selling books, including *Joni, When God Weeps, Joni and Ken*, and the award-winning *A Spectacle of Glory*, and is an internationally known advocate for persons with disabilities. Joni served on the National Council on Disability under two United States presidents and on the US State Department's Disability Advisory Committee. She and Ken have been married for more than thirty years. For more information on Joni and Friends, visit www.joniandfriends.org.

A Spectacle of Glory

God's Light Shining through
Me Every Day

Joni Eareckson Tada
with Larry Libby

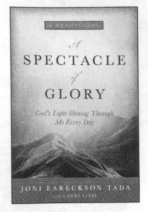

Do you ever wonder why God created
you? The Bible spells it out plainly: God
created you to showcase His glory—to
enjoy it, display it, and demonstrate it every day to all those you
encounter.

After fifty years of living as a quadriplegic, and dealing with
chronic pain on a daily basis, Joni has learned firsthand the im-
portance of glorifying God through the toughest of situations.
Through this devotional, Joni will help you discover how to put
God's glory on display—how to say no to complaining and say
yes to daily following God down even the most difficult paths.
Along the way, you will find great comfort and encouragement
by focusing on the One who longs to lead and guide you every
step of the way, every day.

Don't ever think your life is too ordinary, your world too small,
or your work too insignificant. All of it is a stage set for you to
glorify God.

Available in stores and online!

Joni & Ken

An Untold Love Story

Ken & Joni Eareckson Tada
with Larry Libby

God's immeasurable *grace*. It's the most important ingredient for the perfect love story.

Ken Tada underestimated the challenges of marrying a woman with quadriplegia. Even the honeymoon wasn't easy. Through their years together, Ken became increasingly overwhelmed by the unceasing demands of caring for a woman with chronic, extreme, nightmarish pain. He sinks into depression. Though living under the same roof, they drift apart.

In the midst of their deepest struggles with depression and pain, Ken and Joni return to the one true answer to their struggles. One that is far from a denial of Joni's diagnosis or thoughts of how wonderful a quick exit to heaven would be. In their darkest hour, Ken and Joni encounter a heavenly visitation that changes their lives—and maybe yours—forever.

Joni

An Unforgettable Story

Joni Eareckson Tada

This is the award-winning story of a young woman who triumphed over devastating odds to touch countless lives the world over with the healing message of Christ.

It was more than a hot July afternoon on the Chesapeake Bay. For Joni Eareckson Tada, it was a moment in eternity. In a split second, a diving accident transformed her life from that of a vivacious young woman to one that would be lived for the rest of her days from a wheelchair.

From that tragic beginning has emerged one of the most remarkable stories of our time—the story of faith's triumph over hardship and suffering that is *Joni*. Now more than forty years since its first publication, with more than five million copies in print and translated into fifty languages, *Joni* continues to inspire countless readers worldwide with its message of courage, hope, and grace. This latest edition includes a new foreword by Francis Chan, a new sixteen-page photo insert, an all-new afterword, and an updated resource section.

Available in stores and online!